THE OLD SOUTH

THE OLD SOUTH

MALLARD PRESS

An Imprint of BDD Promotional Book Company
666 Fifth Avenue
New York, N.Y. 10103

MALLARD PRESS

MALLARD PRESS
An imprint of
BDD Promotional Book Company, Inc.
666 Fifth Avenue
New York, NY 10103

Mallard Press and its accompanying design and logo are
trademarks of BDD Promotional Book Company, Inc.

First published in the United States of America
in 1990 by Mallard Press

Printed and bound in Spain

ISBN 0-792-45232-1

Authors: Bennet and Else Daniels
Producer: Solomon M. Skolnick
Designer: Ann-Louise Lipman
Editor: Joan E. Ratajack
Production Coordinator: Valerie Zars
Picture Researcher: Edward Douglas
Editorial Assistant: Carol Raguso
Assistant Picture Researcher: Robert V. Hale

Title page: A century and a quarter after the formal dissolution of the Confederate States of America, the Stars and Bars is still a powerful symbol of romance, honor, and majesty. Preceding pages: The sun rising over a site along the Altamaha River in southern Georgia where Highlanders recruited by James Oglethorpe protected the fledgling colony from attack, illuminates a moment in history and a timeless image of the South's natural beauty.

TABLE OF CONTENTS

INTRODUCTION

From the start, the South was different.

The lush, verdant land had its own distinctive look, the pungent oleander and heliotrope a perfume like nowhere else in America, the warmth of the seasons a unique feel on the skin. Nature and history conspired to make this a region apart, one where tradition plays a more important role, where the past informs every day.

Annie Dillard, author of the acclaimed *Pilgrim at Tinker Creek,* writes of the sweet smell of the virgin South which the earliest explorers encountered long before landfall. "Europe had nothing like it: richly mixed hardwoods all in flower, from the salt coast to the distant interior plains. Giovanni da Verrazano was a hundred leagues off the North Carolina shore when he smelled the great woods—'the sweetest odors.' Raleigh's settlers, approaching the continent on which they would plant the first English colony, smelled the blossoming land of the southern coast: they 'felt a most delicate sweet smell, though they saw no land.'"

The earliest settlers in the South were notably different from the men and women who colonized the land farther north. They were Cavaliers. In the seventeenth century, when Britain was wracked by deep dissensions, the reformers, the free-thinkers, the sober-sided middle-class merchants—in our terms, the Puritans—disputed the very soul of the nation with the Cavaliers, the aristocrats, the upholders of the king, the believers in pomp and ceremony and tradition. These differing attitudes continued as the two camps established beachheads in the New World, bolstered in the South by the strong influence of equally aristocratic French and Spanish explorers.

The citizens of the South today have an affection for the area that goes beyond regional pride to a deep feeling that it is the region that gives them strength and identity. For them, the Old South lives. It is not a collection of long-ago events learned from history books, but a vital part of their personal heritage.

A generation ago, one son of the South, Hodding Carter, the gifted editor of the *Delta Democrat-Times* of Greenville, Mississippi, tried to explain the feeling: "I cannot travel through the valley of Virginia nor along the Mississippi without experiencing a quickening of the blood; if my sons or even strangers are with me, my tongue loosens and I want to tell them of the people who settled and fought and clung there, for they were my people; and if the allegiance is sentimental it is not shallow. I understand the forces that fashioned these men. I am at home with their spirits."

Carter insisted that, "No other section has, to such a degree as does the South, the unity of deep-rooted homogeneity, nor does this unity find elsewhere so uniform an outward expression." One looks to the soul rather than the brain to find the source of this unity.

As early as the 1830's, historical societies had been founded in dozens of towns throughout the South. They organized local celebrations of the anniversaries of battles or other pivotal events, celebrations that reveled in the Cavalier past and instilled in the young a sense of the special southern contribution to the nation's history. "Through monuments, patriotic societies, songs, verse, memorial celebrations, and informal reminiscing, they kept before southern youth the glorious yesteryear," writes historian John Hope Franklin. To this day, patriotic societies thrive.

So it is not happenstance that so much of the Old South is with us still. With booming cities pushing up skyscrapers and modern agribusiness transforming the landscape, the states of the Confederacy still cling to what went before. They preserve vast pockets of the outdoors as they were in the days when only Native Americans lived here; they lovingly restore grand homes and public buildings. This evidence of the past is a vital component of their life today. And it is a vivid reminder of the history of this place.

It has meaning for us no matter where we live. Richard N. Goodwin, an assistant to President Lyndon B. Johnson, noted 20 years ago that in the southern states "the roots of culture and tradition strike deep into our country's past. They yield a sense of continuity, places where the generations are born, remain, and die, in the midst of the frantic, rootless motion that characterizes so much of American life. This sense of place, of belonging, is, I am convinced, why so much of the best in American culture—from Jefferson of Virginia to Faulkner of Mississippi—has flowered on Southern soil." This book is part of the contemporary realization that we can all be enriched by looking back at that tradition.

A Brief History

1513-1765

The South is the only region in the United States with two coasts. That distinction is key to its early history, for it was explored not in a single drive westward from the pioneers' beachhead but in a variety of directions from a variety of beginning points. In 1513, more than a century before the landing of the *Mayflower,* Juan Ponce de León pushed up from Puerto Rico and discovered Florida. Other Spanish explorers followed, driving northward up the peninsula. Hernando de Soto set up an encampment near what is now Tallahassee, and it was there that Christmas was celebrated for the first time on the North American continent.

In 1562, the French established a short-lived colony in South Carolina, and two years later they made a more successful foray into the New World by building in northern Florida the settlement named Fort Caroline, a home for 300 Huguenots led by René de Laudonniére. The Spanish responded by sending a fleet under Don Pedro Menéndez de Avilés to set up their own first permanent colony there, St. Augustine. It glories in its distinction as the oldest American city. Modern visitors can walk the walls of the Castillo de San Marcos, the fortress begun by the Spanish in 1672 and still, with its 13-foot-thick walls constructed of a mixture of sand and ground shells, the dominant structure overlooking Matanzas Bay.

In 1584, after his half-brother Humphrey Gilbert was lost coming back to England from America, Walter Raleigh took up his task of colonizing the New World for Queen Elizabeth. He settled on Albemarle Sound in what is now South Carolina as the optimum first site and established a colony on Roanoke Island. Unprepared for the rigors of the wild frontier, the Raleigh colonists quit Roanoke after a year, sailing back to Britain with the fleet of Francis Drake.

Raleigh tried again the next year, sending 117 men, women, and children to Roanoke. But the Spanish control of the seas kept the British from sending further supplies to the Carolina colonists, and the entire settlement disappeared. Today it is memorable for us as the birthplace of Virginia Dare, the first child born in North America of English parents.

When King James reached a peace accord with Spain in 1606, however, the new freedom for the English to roam the seas renewed interest in colonizing America. One group of would-be settlers, operating under a royal charter giving it the right to all the land from New Jersey to the southern tip of Georgia, loaded three ships led by the *Susan Constant* and headed across the Atlantic. The convoy sailed up the James River and began the village of Jamestown in what is now Virginia.

At first the hardships of the wilderness seemed to dictate for Jamestown a fate like that of Roanoke. John Smith, the military commander of the 144-person group, wrote back to England: "God (being angry with us) plagued us with such famine and sickness that the living were scarce able to bury the dead: our want of sufficient and good victuals, with continual watching, four or five each night at three bulwarks, being the chief cause: only of sturgeon we had great store, whereon our men would so greedily surfeit as it cost many their lives."

The local Indians prevented the colonists' starvation by bringing them corn. Then, at the most desperate moment, a supply ship arrived, offering salvation.

Economic self-sufficiency followed, based on a method of curing tobacco so it would last the journey back to buyers in Britain. It was John Rolfe who first introduced the regular cultivation of the crop in the Jamestown settlement. King James campaigned against the increasing popularity of smoking, calling tobacco "loathsome to the eye, hateful to the nose, harmful to the brain, and dangerous to the lungs." But people were pleased to have all the New World could supply.

Rolfe played a major role in the image as well as the economy of the fledgling Virginia colony. In 1614, he married the Indian princess Pocahontas, daughter of Chief Powhatan, whose generosity had kept the settlers alive in their darkest days. The Rolfes traveled to London, where Pocahontas—taking the name Rebecca—was a public sensation and sparked widespread interest in the Virginia experiment.

The colony prospered, and the settlers were given 100 acres each as their private property. The military ruled the colony in the earliest years, but in 1619, the first seeds of democratic self-government were sown when the army was supplanted by the House of Burgesses, a legislative assembly of well-to-do merchants. The economy was sound; that year 40,000 pounds of tobacco were shipped to London. Glimpses into the very early years of the tobacco economy are available at Flowerdew, one of the earliest plantations, where cultivation began in 1618. A replica of the original windmill of 1621, with its grist house some 10 feet above the field, is there grinding grain on windy days and the fruits of extensive archaeological digs on the site are on display in the museum.

By the 1630's the wealthy enjoyed brick houses, and Jamestown had a brick church. The tower of that church is still standing today, the only structure extant from the original Jamestown. But the National Park Service has faithfully reconstructed thatched-roof mud houses like the ones in which Smith's settlers lived, as well as replicas of the three small ships in which they sought out their new life in America.

As Jamestown grew stronger, the more venturesome Virginians traveled south. Just across the James River from Jamestown, Arthur Allen in 1665 built a brick house—which is still welcoming visitors—displaying Flemish gables accented by unusual triple chimneys at each end of the principal wing. Others moved on to settle near Raleigh's Roanoke site. Charleston, South Carolina, was founded in 1670, under a constitution envisioning a relatively rigid class society, with landowning aristocrats at the top—a very different vision from that which had taken hold in New England. The hospitable climate encouraged huge land-holdings. In 1686, for instance, the still-standing plantation house Medway was built near Charleston; from it 48,000 acres were administered.

The French, meanwhile, who in 1659 had crossed Lake Superior into Wisconsin, began to probe south from there. Jacques Marquette, a Jesuit priest, and Louis Joliet traveled down the Mississippi into Arkansas in 1673; building on their discoveries, René-Robert Cavelier, sieur de La Salle, sailed down the great river to the Gulf of Mexico. Giving the whole Mississippi valley the name Louisiana, he planted French flags there—the beginning of the third European culture that was to shape the old South. French forts followed at such key natural harbors as Biloxi and Mobile.

La Salle gave to his close friend Henri de Tonty trading concessions along the Mississippi, and in 1686 de Tonty built an outpost at the confluence of the Mississippi and Arkansas rivers which, for almost a century, was to be a haven for French explorers. Another of La Salle's lieutenants, Henri Joutel, wrote of how, the following year, a party he was leading, foot-sore and hungry from their trek along the Arkansas, came upon de Tonty's settlement: "Looking over to the further side we discovered a great cross, and at a small distance from it a house built after the French fashion. It is easy to imagine what inward joy we conceived at the sight of that emblem of our salvation. We knelt down, lifting our eyes to heaven, to return thanks to the Divine Goodness for having conducted us so happily, for we made no question of finding French on the other side of the river."

The same year that de Tonty founded his post, an agricultural revolution—and resulting prosperity—came to South Carolina. That year the first seed rice was imported from Madagascar by an imaginative horticulturist, Dr. Henry Woodward, and the Carolina growing conditions proved so hospitable to the crop that planters soon had flooded every bit of land they could use. In just ten years, production had burgeoned to the point where there were barely enough ships to carry it. Rice cultivation required great capital because the fields had to be flooded two or three times a year, a process that involved raising a levee, damming a stream, and making a reservoir. Those who had the wherewithal to undertake such a task established family fortunes, creating with their earnings the great houses that made a showplace of Charleston; it was to these town homes, built with balconies to catch the sea breezes, that they retreated during the summer months.

But the leading crop in the New World was still tobacco, a crop notorious for wearing out the land. The need to find new, fertile acreage encouraged farmers to fell the trees and push their cultivation farther from the coast. As the frontier moved west, the original settlements took on more and more the trappings of established havens of European civilization. For the southern colonies, perhaps no other event symbolized this transition as well as the founding, in 1693, of the College of William and Mary. Two years later, it opened its doors in Williamsburg, and four years after that the town was designated the capital of Virginia.

As the eighteenth century dawned in the New World, Americans were reminded of how much they were still adjuncts of Europe. No longer were the southern colonists all of English stock: French Huguenots, Swiss, and Germans had all settled there, looking for religious freedom. But they were all pulled into the War of the Spanish Succession, with Florida a battleground where Carolinians fought for England against an alliance of Spanish and French troops. The outcome of the hostilities, however, did little to give any of the combatants title to the southern lands; in fact, it encouraged rival attempts at colonization.

In 1718, the French founded New Orleans and, with that city as a base, they made settlements elsewhere on the coast and in the interior. The French managed more than a decade of peace with the indigenous Indians, then got embroiled in the ten-year Natchez War. Today we can get an accurate feel for the period at the reconstructed Fort Condé in Mobile, started by the French in 1824. Guides dressed as French soldiers of the period fire reproductions of eighteenth-century cannons through the ramparts, and actual artifacts from the Natchez War period are arrayed in the museum.

The entanglement of the Natchez War left the English free to establish centers on lands that the French might otherwise have occupied, especially in Georgia. James Oglethorpe, armed with a royal charter, established Savannah as the cornerstone of the new colony. In London, Georgia was conceived of as a buffer zone that would keep the French in the Gulf Coast ports and the Spanish in peninsular Florida from fighting with each other. It was to be the final colony established by the British in America.

Oglethorpe hoped to make the new colony a haven for the unfortunate of England. He and his 20 associates who held the charter for Georgia sought not wealth for themselves, but a way for the urban poor to forge a new life in the New World. They proposed to provide settlers with the necessities of life. But in return for their generosity, they set strict standards of conduct—no rum or brandy allowed; to retain their use of land, settlers had to follow the rules. A town plan was drawn up for Savannah that envisioned a neat checkerboard of houses stretching back from the harbor, surrounded by uncleared forest land. For protection, the settlers were expected to locate near each other. The economic core of the colony was supposed to be silk production, but the white mulberry trees on which silkworms feed never took to the red Georgia soil.

Other colonial legislatures encouraged settlers to push westward from the Atlantic coast by giving free land—or by selling it at prices that amounted to an irresistible bargain. The goal of the policy was economic expansion, but it had political ramifications as well: as Americans made their homes farther from the Atlantic Ocean that linked them to the Old World, they came to think of themselves less as an appendage of Europe and more as an independent nation.

At the same time, in the older communities, the South was prospering, building plantation houses that even today inspire awe. Often, mahogany imported from the West Indies was used for paneling, or Chinese tapestries covered the walls. Adapting to the warm southern temperatures, builders often opted to cover the brick exteriors with stucco in pastel tints: pink, yellow, green, or blue. The rooms were large and airy, to provide a cool haven in the southern summer. Local cabinetmakers, many trained in London, worked in walnut and fruitwoods.

On the grounds of Clemson University in South Carolina, the impressive Hanover House has today found a home, moved there from its original site on the west branch of the Cooper River, now flooded by man-made Lake Moultrie. Hanover House was built in 1716 by Paul de St. Julien on a 1,000-acre tract given to his grandfather by the original holders of the royal charter. Built between massive chimneys which take up most of each side of the house, Hanover's furnishings show the French Huguenot heritage of its builder, especially in the crewelwork curtains and decorated soffits. More typically English is Berkeley; on Virginia's James River, it was the family seat of the Harrisons, the family that gave the United States two presidents. Just a few miles to the east, William Byrd II built the much grander Westover, the center of a 179,000-acre agricultural enterprise. That's more than one-quarter the size of Rhode Island!

Orton Plantation near Wilmington, North Carolina, was begun in 1735 by the sons of a governor of South Carolina, James Moore. One of the boys, Maurice, had been the leader of a band of scions of establishment families who pulled away from their fathers' homes and set up new settlements along the Cape Fear River. The home begun by Maurice and Roger Moore is set behind two-story-high Doric columns, amid cascades of azalea bushes and trees hung with Spanish moss.

The lovely Orton plantings pale beside those of Middleton Place in Charleston. Begun in 1741 by Henry Middleton, who would later become the first chief executive of this nation when he assumed the presidency of the First Continental Congress, the decade-long project produced floral *allées* leading to ornamental lakes and terraced lawns, with a sun-dial garden created around a magnificent thousand-year-old oak. War and earthquake leveled the Tudor-style mansion in which the Middletons once lived, but the plantation today greets visitors with massed azaleas, vivid wild roses climbing live oaks festooned with Spanish moss, and magnolias around twin lakes shaped like butterfly wings. These are the oldest landscaped gardens in America, and the location where the first camellias were planted in the American South—bushes that still bloom every spring.

"It was life upon the plantation, isolated as it was, which shaped the character of the Southern planter and differentiated him from the English yeoman or the English squire," according to historian Thomas Jefferson Wertenbaker in his classic, *The Old South.* "It gave him a sense of security, of self-reliance, of dignity, of responsibility. He must be an agriculturalist, business man, perhaps doctor, builder, blacksmith, cooper. . . . He must be a despot of a little community, a benevolent despot usually, but one upon whose shoulders fell the responsibility for the welfare of ten or twenty or perhaps a hundred human beings."

These planters lived a civilized life. They hired musicians from Europe, studied foreign languages, kept up with the news of the world that so keenly affected their export trade. Every plantation had its own dock, which received imported manufactured goods directly from London. Because the main thrust of the ocean trade was to take American tobacco to England, freight rates for merchandise being brought westward—even large pieces of furniture or heavy, elegant coaches—were set at a minimal level.

"When there were no big-city amusements, and neighbors might be several hours' horseback ride away, men of lively minds turned to books," writes historian Daniel J. Boorstin, former Librarian of Congress. "In 1744, for example, William Byrd's collection of more than 3,600 titles was one of the two or three largest private libraries in North America. Every plantation had at least a small collection of books—manuals of farming, religion, law, medicine, and politics for men who had to run their own small world."

Despite the merchandise trade, that world seemed increasingly isolated from Europe. "Getting a message from England to a colony was complicated," Boorstin notes. "If no ship was sailing, no message could go. The Governor of North Carolina, for example, normally received his communications by way of Virginia. In June, 1745, the Board of Trade in London wrote Governor Johnson of North Carolina complaining that it had received no letter from him in the past three years. A full year later he replied from North Carolina that their letter had only just reached him."

Elsewhere in North Carolina, however, as throughout the South, the settlers who had pressed westward from the Atlantic were living a life much simpler than that of the planters and royal governors. Not much physical evidence exists for today's pilgrims to see, but an exception is the restored Moravian village of Old Salem in what is now the bustling center of cigarette manufacturing, Winston-Salem. The town was forged out of the wilderness in 1766 by German immigrants moving south from Pennsylvania.

The Moravians prized education and founded in Salem the first college for women in the South. They also believed that people best found God by associating with those in similar circumstances, so married couples had their own circle and the single men and women each stayed in their own groups. The Single Brothers House is today one of the centers of Old Salem, for that is where visitors can see demonstrations of the crafts practiced in the mid-eighteenth century that made Old Salem a self-sufficient community.

But self-sufficiency can only go so far, and again the southern colonists were pulled into a war between England and Spain, and Oglethorpe, rather than serving as a peace-keeper, allied his Georgians with the Creek Indians and invaded Spanish Florida. The Spanish tried to retaliate by driving north into Georgia, but they were repulsed.

The French, however, were adding to the cultural mix in the South. In 1755 the Acadians were deported from Nova Scotia, and bands of them made their way to Louisiana, establishing Cajun communities that more than two centuries later preserve their distinctive speech, music, cooking, and culture.

The French and Indian War was raging on Virginia's western frontier and throughout much of the North. When England, France, and Spain finally sat down in Paris in 1763 to end the battles, England came away as the undisputed

ruler of the colonies east of the Mississippi River. Spain lost its claim to Florida, but in return it got from the French the city of New Orleans and the Mississippi valley land west of the mighty river originally claimed by La Salle.

1765-1820

Throughout the period of exploration, the colonists identified themselves first with their own settlements and second with the European country from which they—or their predecessors—had come. But with the end of the French and Indian War and the attempts by the British Parliament to extract more wealth from America, the colonists began to forge links among themselves, to feel that they were Americans. While large cities had developed in the North, the South (except for glittering Charleston) was still primarily rural: the largest city in Virginia—the capital, Williamsburg—had fewer than 2,000 residents. But increasingly the citizens of the New World saw that these differences were less important than the goal they had in common.

They were unified in their increasing chafing under British authority, objecting, for instance, to the law requiring them to provide housing for British soldiers and rum for British sailors. Among the 13 British colonies, four that would later join the Confederacy sent delegates to New York City in October 1765, to a congress convened especially to protest the institution of tax stamps on all commercial paper.

It was the northern colonies that had been hardest hit by England's initial drive to extract more revenue from the New World. But the 1764 Currency Act, prohibiting all the colonies from issuing legal tender, affected the South as well and engendered a new anger with the rulers across the sea. "These tenders in law have been our property for ages past and cannot with any color of justice be taken from us," complained South Carolina merchant Henry Laurens.

Virginians were especially vocal in their demands that the people elect the government, a political philosophy that stemmed from the colony's success for well over a century with the House of Burgesses.

But during the 1760's, the most radical opposition to the established government came from the western frontiersmen, who complained not only of the British oppression but also of the fact that they had no representation in colonial legislatures, which were made up of delegates from the more settled coastal areas. Often the complaints boiled over into violent demonstrations. Richard Henderson, sitting as a judge, fumed after witnessing such a riot in Hillsborough, North Carolina, that the settlers "are abandoned to every principle of virtue and desperately engaged . . . in the most shocking barbarities. . . ."

In 1769, these frontiersmen, acting as vigilantes, won major concessions in South Carolina, including the creation of local courts. The following year, their counterparts in North Carolina were routed at the Battle at Almanac Creek. But win or lose, the colonists were learning that it might be necessary to take up arms to win the political liberty they were increasingly claiming as their due.

Committees of Correspondence were formed in virtually every town to press for those freedoms, and each of the colonies except for Georgia sent delegates to the 1774 Continental Congress in Philadelphia, a body without any real power but of great symbolic importance as a unified, national voice for the colonists in their dealings with London. The spirit of revolution was contagious: in Edenton, North Carolina, in what was the first American political action organized exclusively by women, the wives of the town gathered in the square to swear to stop making, serving, or drinking tea as long as the British tax was in effect.

The next year, in his famous "Give me liberty or give

me death" speech, Patrick Henry openly warned that military battles would be unavoidable. Before the end of the year, his prediction had come true, as British armies and American militia clashed up and down the Atlantic seaboard. Virginians drove out the royal governor, who left Norfolk in flames behind him.

Skirmishes continued. At Moore's Creek Bridge, North Carolina, for instance, in early 1776 an estimated 1,100 revolutionaries defeated a significantly larger force assembled by the colonial governor. With the defeat of the Tories, the British warships that had planned to land at Cape Fear turned back. Colonists elsewhere proceeded to prepare for war. At Charleston they built Fort Moultrie, whose new defensive ramparts gave the locals the necessary vantage point to repel a British naval attack in late June.

The non-British national strains that had already added so much diversity to the southern settlements gained in political and economic importance: France and Spain fanned the flames of revolution by providing money and equipment.

To push the Continental Congress in Philadelphia to take a decisive step, Virginia delegate Richard Henry Lee introduced a resolution that the colonies be recognized as independent states. Lee's resolution passed on July 2, 1776, and two days later the group took the final step of approving the Declaration of Independence.

The British, willing to make virtually any concession to the colonists but the one they most demanded — independence — fought hard. They took Savannah in 1778, stifling dissent in Georgia. In the spring of 1780, they were back at Charleston, and this time the attack was successful. The South Carolina port became the seat of a new American government loyal to King George, and the home base for forays against the revolutionaries throughout the Carolinas.

At the same time, the British also took control of Augusta, Georgia, renaming the fort in honor of General Charles Cornwallis and repelling later American attempts to dislodge them. (Today the site of the fort is the churchyard of St. Paul's Episcopal Church.) With fighting raging on so many fronts, the Spanish, taking advantage of the British preoccupation with the war, reestablished their own dominion over some areas previously controlled by King George, including the region around Natchez.

By the following year, however, the revolutionaries had organized their southern forces under General Nathanael Greene, and managed to push the British out of the Carolinas. Cornwallis tried to recoup at a new headquarters in Yorktown, Virginia. That became the final battleground of the war, and General George Washington led his troops southward from Long Island to assemble in Williamsburg, 16,000 strong. They pinched Cornwallis, with a far smaller force, from the north and the French fleet sailed up Chesapeake Bay to help with a merciless siege of the town.

Today visitors can still see the cannonballs embedded in the walls of the home of General Thomas Nelson, which had been commandeered as Cornwallis's headquarters. Also restored is the Moore family home, where two of Cornwallis's officers sat down on October 18, 1781, with Colonel John Laurens, representing the American troops, and the vicomte de Noailles, the French delegate, to draw up the 14-point "Articles of Capitulation." The next day, it was signed by Cornwallis and Washington, and the British troops formally laid down their arms in a pasture south of Yorktown now known as Surrender Field — just 23 miles from the Jamestown site of the first permanent English settlement in the New World.

It took two more years for the governments to agree to the terms of an official peace treaty, but from the moment of the Cornwallis surrender — as the military band played a tune entitled "The World Turned Upside Down" — the southern colonies were colonies no more but part of an independent nation. The terms of the peace treaty did, however, greatly affect the part of the region not included among the 13 colonies. Britain officially gave Spain control of Florida and the key Mississippi port of New Orleans; the home built in New Orleans for the first Spanish governor is still standing in the Vieux Carré at 529 Royal Street.

With hostilities behind them, the states focused on building a better life for their citizens. One key was learning: in 1785, the University of Georgia was founded, the first nondenominational state-run institution of higher education in the country. Still in use on its campus in Athens are some of the earliest buildings. In the same year, Congress, operating under the Articles of Confederation, set up rules for the sale at auction of land on the western frontier, stipulating that 640 acres in each township of 36 square miles should be used to support public elementary education.

The new better life for Americans was to be based on freedom, and Virginia led the way. In 1786, the legislature adopted a statute, proposed by Thomas Jefferson, declaring that the government had no right to impose any doctrinaire religious beliefs on the populace or to cause any person to "suffer on account of his religious opinions or belief."

But Virginians and their fellow southerners were becoming increasingly disenchanted with the loose central government of the young nation. At a special Constitutional Convention called in Philadelphia to amend the Articles of Confederation, they pressed for something more sweeping: an entirely reorganized government, with a strong executive branch, national courts, and a two-house legislature, where representation would be based on each state's population and wealth.

That Virginia proposal, first set forth on May 29, 1787, was too radical for the delegates, but it formed the framework for the compromise that followed — a Constitution that carefully balanced the powers of the large and small states, the local legislatures and the central government, the judges and lawmakers and administrators. By the middle of the next year, the states had accepted the new Constitution, and the Confederation Congress officially declared itself a thing of the past. Maryland and Virginia each gave up land along the Potomac to form an independent district to be the capital of the new government, although it would be another ten years before the marshy new capital was developed enough for Congress to actually meet there.

By unanimous vote of the 69 electors, Virginia's George Washington was elected president of the new nation, and less than three months later — on April 30, 1790 — he took up the reins of office.

It was a yeasty period where revolutionary ideas were not confined solely to the realm of politics. The history of the South in the decades ahead was as much affected by technological change as it was by political change. The invention of the cotton gin in 1793 had a profound effect on the economy of the South. The device, for which Eli Whitney was awarded one of the new nation's first patents in 1794, efficiently separates the seeds and the fibers in the cotton boll. It greatly increased the demand for the crop. The cotton gin in use today is not dramatically different from that first marketed by Whitney. Stop by Clio, South Carolina, any working day in the fall and see it in operation. Or seek out the Plantation Agriculture Museum in Scott, Arkansas, where both nineteenth-century and modern versions of the invention are on display. At Lewis-Turnout, South Carolina, visitors in October and November can go into the billowy fields and pick their own cotton.

The ability of gins to handle enormous quantities of cotton changed the economics of plantation life, making feasible bigger and bigger operations and demanding large

This page, above: *Throughout the South, monuments to the heroes of the past keep their exploits alive and inspire each new generation of citizens.* Below: *From a rude beginning, reproduced at Jamestown, Virginia, intrepid colonists created a great nation.* Opposite: *Replicas of the cramped and precarious English sailing ships in which the early settlers crossed the Atlantic allow modern Americans to appreciate the bravery and hope out of which the country was formed.*

This page: *The first European families in the New World founded Jamestown, Virginia, in 1607. Although barely 60 people survived, in less than a decade they had created the first democratically elected governing council in the Americas. Opposite: At the end of the seventeenth century, the seat of Virginia's colonial government was moved from Jamestown to Williamsburg, where this palatial residence was built for the royal governor. Overleaf: Thanks to loving restoration and reproduction, Williamsburg lives on as a colonial town, where the authentic buildings are complemented by costumed townspeople who go through the routines of a typical eighteenth-century day.*

numbers of laborers to clear previously forested land and to plant and harvest the new fields. Even before the cotton gin the economic attitudes of the South and North had diverged: in 1790 Patrick Henry gained attention with his remonstrance against the fiscal policies of the Federalists, claiming that having the central government assume the debts run up by the individual colonies during the war would lead to the "prostration of agriculture at the feet of commerce."

In *The Growth of the American Republic,* the standard American history text for an entire generation of students, Samuel Eliot Morison and Henry S. Commager wrote, "American political history until 1865 is largely the story of the rival interests, capitalist and agrarian, Northern and Southern, contending for the control of the government."

But the massive farming enterprises developed to feed the cotton gin's capacity would worsen the gulf. Increasingly, northerners became advocates of an economic policy that used taxes to discourage imports and encourage domestic manufacturing while southern politicians argued for low tariffs, so dependent was their welfare on international trade.

In the years immediately after the Revolutionary War, the new nation prospered and pushed westward and settlers flowed into new lands as soon as rough paths through the forests were cleared. The cotton trade promised markets for all the cotton the planters could grow. By 1796, there were enough residents in Tennessee for the area to be admitted to the union as the sixteenth state, the first southern addition to the original colonies. Two years later, the fledgling Congress officially established the territory of Mississippi, which included what is now that state as well as Alabama.

Some years before, Georgia, with claims on land as far as the Mississippi River, had sold more than 25 million acres of its undeveloped western reaches—land in what is now the states of Mississippi and Alabama—to a group of pioneering developers. Georgia's right to dispose of the property was a matter of great controversy, since both indigenous Indians and the Spanish also had arguably legitimate claims.

The expansionist plans of the new owners led to war threats from Spain, but a confrontation was averted and Spain came to realize that it would never achieve its dreams of a major colony in North America. In the 1795 Treaty of San Lorenzo, Spain gave U.S. citizens authority to navigate the Mississippi and to store merchandise at its mouth in New Orleans warehouses. Five years later, Spain secretly ceded to France all of its rights to the land along the Mississippi. The heritage of those years remains, however: in Natchez, for example, the local garden club has preserved a home from the late eighteenth century, a gem of Spanish provincial architecture with elaborately carved mantels and a two-story-high gallery running across the entire front.

The Spanish realization of the difficulties of holding on to North American properties in the face of the zesty growth of the United States soon impressed itself on Napoleon too. He decided that his New World ambitions were futile, and in late 1802, he suddenly offered to sell the entire colony of Louisiana—stretching from New Orleans almost to the Canadian border—to the United States. For a total of $15 million in federal bonds and indemnifications of France against claims from Americans, the United States doubled in size, although the offer and acceptance were so unexpected that at the time of the deal there was no firm agreement on just what land was included. There was no doubt, however, that what are now known as Louisiana and Arkansas were included in the purchase.

To the Federalist forces of the North, the new land seemed likely to lead to a political alliance of southern and western Americans, which would upset the existing balance between the two parties and give President Thomas Jefferson and his backers something like a permanent majority.

One result of the imprecision in the terms of the Louisiana Purchase was a continuing confusion over the legal status of the Gulf Coast. Although settlers from the states had poured into the crescent, Spain continued to insist that the entire stretch was part of its colony of Florida, that it had not been included in its 1800 grant of North American holdings to France, and that therefore France could not have sold it to the United States. But in 1810 President James Madison announced publicly that he interpreted the terms of the Louisiana Purchase to include what was then called West Florida. The Americans there—making up 90 percent of the population—immediately reacted by seizing the Spanish fort at Baton Rouge. Madison annexed the entire stretch east from there to Pensacola, but despite his promulgation the Spaniards continued in control of their battlements in Mobile.

The West Florida episode was typical of the increasing restiveness on the part of Americans, especially those in the South and West, toward European interference with the new nation. John C. Calhoun of South Carolina was one of these young Americans, called War Hawks. Elected to Congress in 1811, his agitation against British hampering of U.S. ships finally persuaded Congress the following year to declare war against Great Britain. It was a move that immediately laid bare festering regional factions: Connecticut and Massachusetts flatly refused to support the war and hinted that they might pull out of the Union.

The British tried to capitalize on that sentiment by concentrating its naval blockade of U.S. ports on the Gulf and the southern Atlantic cities, drying up trade there while New England docks were busy. The northern states, however, had no intention of going beyond rhetoric to actually splitting the Union, and when London realized that, the blockade was extended up the entire Atlantic coast. In 1814, the British landed troops along Chesapeake Bay; they marched northward, burning Washington but failing to take the fort at Baltimore.

During that campaign, the British and Americans had been discussing terms to end the war, and those talks dragged on through the second half of the year. During the first week of 1815, U.S. troops under Andrew Jackson repulsed the British as they attacked New Orleans, providing the young nation with its most glorious military victory. But by then the peace negotiators in Belgium had already signed a treaty ending the hostilities.

The Treaty of Ghent changed very little, yet the United States that emerged from the War of 1812 was set on a course of regional confrontation that would only worsen over the next half-decade.

The South was growing. Louisiana became a state in 1812, and Mississippi joined the Union five years later. Alabama was broken off from Mississippi and established as a separate territory, but only two years later it too became a state.

Military escapades by Jackson, not against the British but against the Creek Indians and the Spaniards, had greatly added to the holdings of the southern states by forcing the Indians to turn over huge tracts in Alabama and Georgia and making it seem likely that Spain could be completely ousted from Florida whenever the U.S. military put its mind to it. That happened, again with Jackson at the head of the troops, in 1818, and the following year Spain turned over to the United States all of its claims to the peninsula.

But more central to the developing fissure in the nation was the continuing northern resentment at being plunged into the war in the first place. Huge textile factories were just being established along the rivers of New England, and the economic interests of the North and South took even more divergent courses. New Englanders railed against the slavery that was at the core of the southern economy. Then, in 1816, Congress passed the protective tariff that it had been debating

Above: *The original outbuildings (now rebuilt) on the grounds of the Governor's Palace once served as stables. Below: Members of the resident staff who work at the stables are as well versed in colonial lore as they are in animal care.*

Clockwise from left: When Archibald Blair opened Williamsburg's first tavern in 1735, he named it for Walter Raleigh, evidence that the explorers of a century before had already become icons. The clean, simple lines of Williamsburg's domestic architecture contrast with the imperial style of the government buildings. The rear view of Raleigh Tavern shows what an inviting way station it was; when the British governor dissolved the House of Burgesses, the delegates, including Thomas Jefferson and Patrick Henry, continued their deliberations here.

since its first session, now intended to protect American textile mills from foreign competition.

The tariff was a major loss for the South. In fact, the new economic policy threw the country into a deep three-year depression, leading to the foreclosure of many mortgages in the South. The perilous economic climate brought into the open regional differences that in better times could be patched over. The result, for much of the century, was a divisive battle about the direction of the nation.

1820-1865

The first shots of the Civil War that so decisively separated the historical memory of the Old South from that of the rest of the nation were fired on April 12, 1861, at the Union stronghold at Fort Sumter in Charleston harbor, the only arsenal in South Carolina still in the hands of Federal troops. But as Reuben Davis, who represented Mississippi in both the U.S. and Confederate Congresses noted, "It was the signal for battle, but the troops were marshalled and war declared long before."

In fact the conflagration had crept toward inevitability for the previous four decades as the South and the North had become increasingly estranged over their different economic systems and the issue that had come to symbolize those differences: slavery.

The geographic breach first became written into law in 1820, in the Missouri Compromise, when Congress decided that slavery would be prohibited in territories above latitude 36°30' and allowed south of that line, roughly the dividing line between Virginia and North Carolina.

At the same time, the economic breach widened. If the 1816 tariff law favored northern interests, the 1828 import tax law seemed to the South to go well beyond that to a complete abdication of its interests. Dubbed the "Tariff of Abominations," it hiked the rates on virtually all imports—a decision perceived as so unfair to the South that the South Carolina legislature drew up a formal statement questioning the constitutionality of the measure. The document argued that Congress may not pass any taxes that favor one section over another, and warned that if Congress overstepped its power any individual state might nullify that law. "Feeling it to be their bounden duty to expose and resist all encroachments upon the true spirit of the Constitution," the legislators recorded their "protest against it as unconstitutional, oppressive, and unjust."

That same year, in the first national election in which a broad-based electorate decided the outcome, an all-South ticket was elected: Andrew Jackson went to the White House and Vice-President John C. Calhoun, who had severed ties with his former ally John Quincy Adams, continued in the number two job. The team took over the government as the debate over westward expansion—supposedly quelled by the Missouri Compromise—continued. Again, the Mason-Dixon Line was the dividing point: northerners argued against cheap sales of public lands, and the South favored the policy to spur expansion, but also to limit the power of the central government over states' rights.

As the abolitionist movement grew in the North, the South took a fresh look at the institution of slavery, debating the issue at length in the Virginia legislature in 1831, when an antislavery motion was defeated by a 73-to-58 vote. Many of those voting against the resolution saw no alternative: it was widely assumed in the South that blacks could not be integrated into white society and that relocating the slaves—as southeastern Indians were then being relocated to the West—was impractical.

Disappointing the South, Jackson broke with Calhoun and became a staunch advocate of a strong government in Washington and of high tariffs. After he was reelected in 1832, the South Carolina legislature made good on its threat to nullify the tariff law. A new state law forbade customs officials from collecting the duties. South Carolina threatened to pull out of the Union entirely if Washington disobeyed. Jackson insisted that no state had the power to secede, and sent additional troops to Fort Sumter. Congress acted quickly to defuse the issue, setting up a timetable for gradually reducing tariff levels. The controversy, however, foreshadowed the bigger fissure that was to come.

For the next 30 years, the debate over slavery raged, with the abolitionists finding some of their most effective proponents in southerners who had decided that the practice must be abolished, people like the Grimké sisters of South Carolina and Liberty Party presidential candidate James G. Birney, a former slaveholder from Kentucky. Perhaps their top attraction at antislavery rallies was the fugitive slave Frederick Douglass, an accomplished orator.

A particularly contentious issue was what to do about fugitives such as Douglass; under Federal law they could be pursued and returned, but many northern states passed laws that tried to nullify these statutes by forbidding state officials from helping Federal officials who were going after slaves. Congress stood ready to get tough about enforcing the fugitive slave laws, but only as part of a compromise that would see California admitted to the Union as a nonslave state and the slave trade outlawed in the District of Columbia.

That Compromise of 1850 was hailed by northern commentators at the time as a political masterstroke. But many in the South felt it could not prevent the impending clash of arms. "They have fired cannon in Washington, and displayed lights as if for a great victory," the Charleston *Mercury* editorialized. "Well, it is a victory, a victory over justice and all sound statesmanship. The burning of powder may not stop with Washington."

The South felt its national political power slipping away as the size of the nation grew, and Calhoun revived the threat of secession as the ultimate act if the North allied its interests with the West. "The South asks for justice, simple justice, and less she ought not to take," Calhoun warned. "She has surrendered so much that she has little left to surrender." Like so much of his influential writing, the first draft of that speech was penned at Fort Hill, his home for the final 25 years of his life, now a monument on the campus of South Carolina's Clemson College. The institution itself was founded on acreage donated by Calhoun's son-in-law, and many of the furnishings in Fort Hill today are those owned by Calhoun while Vice-President.

Throughout the period of the bitter political disagreement over the slavery question, the South was prospering. Cotton prices in Britain were hitting new highs. In the mid-1830s, they reached 15 cents a pound—a level that let a planter recoup a 35 percent profit. "The flush days had arrived," writes Harnett T. Kane, whose novels have traced the lives of many of the South's most eminent women. "As never before, the fleecy growth thrived in Georgia, in North and South Carolina. Then at once it proved that it could succeed even more magnificently in the long lowlands of the Deep South, in area after area within reach of the Gulf and the Atlantic.

"Fresh wealth poured out of the earth, in a flow greater than the region has ever known. For those who managed to hold their own on the shifting scene, there was a greater means and a greater opulence. The era was that of the Greek Revival, when white-pillared establishments rose along the banks of the rivers, in the gardens at the end of the fields, and at Natchez, Memphis, Montgomery, and scores of other points about the South."

That architectural style is well preserved today in numerous buildings sheltered by local preservation organizations.

This page, above: *From shops such as this one, visitors can purchase reproductions of artifacts of the pre-Revolutionary South. Below: In the working kitchen of the Governor's Palace, the baking of delicious breads and cakes continues. Opposite: At the cooper's shop, visitors can see how barrels were formed from staves and hoops.*

This page: *Before the development of interchangable parts, eighteenth-century gunsmiths crafted each weapon individually from start to finish.* Opposite: *The contemporary engraving on this gun butt serves as a reminder that the South has always valued the ornate and elegant.*

A notable example is Arlington, set amid oaks and magnolias on a sloping lawn on Cotton Avenue in Birmingham, built around 1850 by a local judge and today furnished with prize examples of nineteenth-century American decorative arts. Another is Chretien Point Plantation near Sunset, Louisiana, a Greek Revival masterpiece that survived a Civil War battle on its grounds; its magnificent staircase was copied for Tara in the film *Gone With the Wind*. The South's cotton wealth showed up in wonderful Greek Revival public buildings, too: the Old Court House in Lynchburg, Virginia, looks as shining and impressive as it did when built in 1855, and today it serves as a museum tracing the history of the area.

The cotton profits also gave southern businessmen the capital for expansion. Alabama and Mississippi had used land grants from the Federal Government to encourage railroads to build links to the West. Typical of the boom that resulted was the growth of Shreveport in the northwest corner of Louisiana. Driftwood had accumulated over the centuries in the Red River, making it impassable for 160 miles. But in the late 1830's Henry Shreve, a determined steamboat entrepreneur, broke his way through, opening a new water highway for cotton commerce and founding the immediately successful town that bears his name.

Sectional tensions worsened in 1857, when the northern states were plunged into a deep depression triggered by wild speculation in land and railroads. The reason Abraham Lincoln got so much national attention from his local speech warning that the nation could not long endure with half opposed to slavery and half endorsing it is that he spoke aloud a prophecy more and more citizens had been realizing silently in their hearts. Two years later, the mad attack led by John Brown on the federal arsenal at Harper's Ferry—a raid intended to spark off a slave revolt in the South—set off waves of fear throughout the South that armed violence was near, even though the foray was quickly quelled and Brown was hanged after his capture by a troop of Marines under Robert E. Lee.

After Lincoln's election in 1860, many in the South thought that a complete sundering of the nation was inevitable. As Jefferson Davis later explained, "No alternative remained except to seek the security out of the Union which they had vainly tried to obtain within it. The hope of our people may be stated in a sentence: it was to escape from injury and strife in the Union, to find prosperity and peace out of it."

Even before the Electoral College met to make Lincoln's victory official, South Carolina convened a secession convention, which declared the contract between that state and the Federal Government dissolved. Within a month, Florida, Georgia, Alabama, Mississippi, Louisiana, and Texas had joined South Carolina in passing formal secession measures, and Federal forts in most of those states had been seized by state militia. Those takeovers were without serious fighting, and all sides worked feverishly to find an alternative to war to solve the deep sectional problems.

The states that had seceded met in early February 1861, in Montgomery, to form the Confederate States of America with Davis as President and a constitution modeled closely on the U.S. Constitution. At the same time, representatives of the southern states were negotiating in Washington a compromise intended to end the impasse. The outline of an agreement was reached—one that would have added to the U.S. Constitution a guarantee that slavery could continue in the states where it was already established—but then, in response to resupply efforts by Washington, the South Carolina troops began the barrage of Fort Sumter that was to go on for 34 hours and make a peaceful resolution impossible. Lincoln immediately deemed an "insurrection" under way and called for a major increase in the size of the Union

army. Virginia seceded two days later and was joined the following month by North Carolina, Tennessee, and Arkansas.

"Hatreds, North and South, had been fanned too long by pro-slavery orators or abolitionists to require any philosophical statement of war aims in 1861," historian Harvey Wish writes. "Volunteers, carried away by patriotic bands, speeches, posters, the kisses or threats of young ladies, and other community pressures, overwhelmed the recruiting stations. Sons of wealthy planters organized cavalry companies under their command. Confederate flags flew on Southern college campuses even before hostilities began, and classrooms emptied quickly, forcing some institutions to close."

The South's military tradition gave it an immediate edge in the fighting. The shooting started in earnest at the first battle of Bull Run in July, where Union hopes of a speedy march to Richmond were dashed and its 35,000 inexperienced troops were routed by the disciplined Confederate army. The next year, the two armies clashed again on the same battlefield, again giving the Confederacy a stunning victory and opening the way for Lee's aggressive incursion into Union territory, begun in September. Today the battlefield at Manassas, Virginia, is a national park where Civil War buffs retrace the skirmishes and a museum exhibits memorabilia of the era and displays the course of the two battles on a giant electronic map.

By the time of the second battle of Bull Run, however, the Union had had time to train its troops and find aggressive generals, and the tide of the war had begun to turn. While Lee pushed North, the Confederate Fort Donelson on the Cumberland River fell to Union troops, giving them Nashville and a western entry point into the Confederacy. Then the blockade of New Orleans was breached and the Union took control of the mouth of the Mississippi. At the eastern edge of the war, the Confederacy lost its main naval base at Norfolk to the Union.

It was a time of deprivation for the South. "We were blockaded at every side, could get nothing from without, so had to make everything at home," Victoria Virginia Clayton, the wife of an Alabama planter, wrote in a postwar reminiscence. "Having been heretofore only an agricultural people, it became necessary for every home to be supplied with spinning wheels and the old-fashioned loom, in order to manufacture clothing for members of the family. This was no small undertaking." Mansions gave up their carpets to provide coverlets for Confederate soldiers; shoes were in such short supply that some fighting men went barefoot; a disrupted transportation system meant that even foodstuffs, which planters' families began growing instead of cotton, were scarce in some parts of the South.

But it was a time of glory, too, tapping the deepest honor of southerners. Plantation houses were turned into hospitals, and the women left behind, defying the strong tradition of chivalry that was supposed to protect mothers and daughters from the harsher tasks of life, volunteered as nurses for the wounded.

During the war, Wish says, "the Confederacy was honored with the finest poetry that Dixieland had yet produced. Her best poets knew the sacrifices and sufferings of army life and drew their themes from the heart and emotions of battle." Henry Timrod and Paul Hamilton Hayne mixed in their works the horror of the war with their lyrical love of the beauty of the mountains, pine forests, and cottonfields of their home region.

The war was made up of thousands of different encounters which were not only seemingly unrelated to each other but at times without even a central focus. As Lee's biographer Burke Davis notes: "Those who begin with the notion that the war took place in Virginia discover that there were more than 5,500 actions, about 95 of them real battles—

Preceding page: *Members of a fife and drum corps hurry through Dr. Barraud's Garden in Williamsburg.* This page, above: *A member of the Williamsburg staff fires a flintlock.* Below: *Crops at Williamsburg are harvested by traditional methods.*

This page, above: *One of the thousands of visitors to Williamsburg is transported back in time.* Below: *Fife and drum corps performances can still send chills of excitement up a listener's spine.* Overleaf: *The Magazine on Duke of Gloucester Street once served as the main arsenal for the entire Virginia colony. With walls 22 inches thick, it has been in continuous use since 1715.*

and that California saw six skirmishes, New Mexico nineteen, Oregon four, with others in Utah, Idaho, and Washington Territory. Land fighting may be traced as far north as St. Albans, Vermont, where there was a Confederate raid; other raiders struck in New York, Illinois, and Minnesota.

"The final action of the war was at the edge of the Arctic Circle. The southernmost sweep of the Union blockade was to a lonely sand spur on the Florida coast destined for later fame as Cape Canaveral."

In the most out-of-the-way corners of the South today there are sites that recall events major and minor in the conflagration. Fort Jefferson, off the tip of Florida in the Dry Tortugas, was a key battlement in the attempt to blockade the Confederacy, and later served as the prison for Dr. Samuel A. Mudd, who set the leg that John Wilkes Booth broke after shooting President Lincoln. At the opposite corner of the Confederacy, at Pea Ridge, in the northwestern corner of Arkansas, a 4,200-acre National Military Park commemorates the 1862 clash of 26,000 troops, a pitched battle where Confederate generals Benjamin McCulloch and William Y. Slack were both killed.

The Union forces won at Pea Ridge. But they failed in their initial efforts to capture the heart of the Confederacy, its capital city of Richmond, Virginia. Richmond had become the capital of the South 15 weeks after Jefferson Davis took the oath of office as President. In 1862, outnumbered by Union troops and suffering heavy casualties, Lee and Stonewall Jackson held the line and saved the city. Such was their military brilliance that many in the North began to question the basic wisdom of the war.

On January 1, 1863, Lincoln issued the Emancipation Proclamation, and the drama of the move pulled together public opinion in the North and galvanized support for the war. The new enthusiasm was translated into battlefield victories: the Union armies were in control of the entire Mississippi River valley by the time the troops won a major victory on July 4 at Gettysburg, Pennsylvania, the northernmost point of the Confederate push. The following year, Sherman began his devastating march from the west, through Georgia to the Atlantic; Savannah fell just three days before Christmas.

But, as poet Stephen Vincent Benét notes, "We could give a list of great battles—Bull Run, Chancellorsville, Antietam, Vicksburg, Gettysburg, Chickamauga. But that does not tell the story. The story was in the hearts of men and women—in the gay recklessness of the Southern cavalry and the stubborn resistance of the Union soldiers."

The end of the South's bold attempt to use the power of the states to curb the authority of the central government in Washington was by then clearly near. Lee surrendered to Grant at Appomattox Court House in Virginia on April 9, 1865. But other elements of the Confederacy fought on. It was another six weeks before the last of the Confederate soldiers laid down their arms. The most significant of those later meetings—General Joseph Johnston's surrender of 90,000 troops to Sherman—took place at the Bennett family homestead near Durham, which has been reconstructed for visitors the way it looked that sad spring.

Take that Banner down! 'tis tattered;
Broken is its staff and shattered;
And the valiant hosts are scattered,
Over whom it floated high.
Oh, 'tis hard for us to fold it,
Hard to think there's none to hold it.
Hard that those who once unrolled it
Now must furl it with a sigh!

So wrote southern poet Abram J. Ryan, a Confederate army chaplain, of the Stars and Bars at the end of the great conflict.

Furl that Banner! True, 'tis gory,
Yet 'tis wreathed around with glory,
And 'twill live in song and story
Though its folds are in the dust!
For its fame on brightest pages,
Penned by poets and by sages,
Shall go sounding down the ages—
Furl its folds though now we must.

PLANTATIONS

Preceding pages: *Washington devoted much of his adult life to the development and expansion of Mount Vernon. The first addition to the original 11-room house was a second floor, reached by this enticing, curved staircase. This page, clockwise from left: Charles Willson Peale's portrait of the young George Washington dominates this sitting room at Mount Vernon. The elegant plaster molding and Palladian windows lavished on the public rooms at Mount Vernon reveal how strongly life in the colonies was influenced by eighteenth-century European styles. The symmetry of the furnishings is amazing because each chair was made individually by hand. Opposite: Objets d'art in the mansion include gifts presented to Washington by foreign heads of state.*

Preceding pages: *Monticello represented a turning point in the architecture of the Old South. It was designed by Jefferson as a villa, a distinct break from the boxy look of homes nearer Virginia's Atlantic shore. This page, above: Jefferson grew more than 250 varieties of vegetables and herbs; continuing cultivation at Monticello shows that the land remains fertile. Below: At his home near Charlottesville, Virginia, begun in 1769, Jefferson began the Greek Revival architectural movement that would dominate public buildings in the Old South for decades to come.*

Above: *By opening the house to the sunlight and by distributing flowers profusely, the guardians of Monticello bring the lush outdoors into the mansion.*
Below: *The writing table designed by Jefferson is among the authentic, original furnishings on display at Monticello.*

Above: *By 1720, settlers had moved to the foothills of the Blue Ridge mountains and had founded Orange, Virginia, the site of James Madison's home, Montpelier. Below: Tuckahoe Plantation, just outside Richmond, "contains some of the most important architectural ideas of the early Georgian period," according to University of Virginia professor Frederick Nichols.*

This page, above: *Treasures collected in Europe by the Randolph family decorate Tuckahoe. Below: Tuckahoe is a living part of the Old South; not just a museum, it continues as the home and working farm it has been for 275 years. Overleaf: Built by English architect John Hawks in 1770 as the residence for the royal governors of Carolina, Tryon Palace in New Bern, North Carolina, was acclaimed by many as the most beautiful building in America.*

This page, above: *10 of the original outbuildings at Boone Hall in Mt. Pleasant, South Carolina, still survive on 738 acres of the original plantation.* Below: *Boone Hall was begun in 1681, but these cabins probably were not built until 50 years later.* Opposite: *"The Avenue of Oaks" at Boone Hall stretches for three-quarters of a mile, and the plantation boasts an historic pecan grove.*

Preceding page: *Facing the Ashley River near Charleston, Drayton Hall is an especially authentic representative of the Old South. Seven generations of the Drayton family lived here without adding such modern touches as electricity, plumbing, or central heating.* This page, above: *Rice and indigo were the main crops on which the prosperity of South Carolina plantations such as Rutledge were built.* Below: *Begun more than 300 years ago, the nearby Magnolia Gardens feature, in addition to wisteria and live oak, 250 varieties of magnolia and 900 of camellia.* Overleaf: *Middleton Place, laid out by Henry Middleton, who later became president of the Continental Congress, boasts terraces, parterres, and a string of ornamental lakes.*

These pages: *23 ornate Corinthian columns are all that remain of Windsor, the great mansion built just before the Civil War near Port Gibson, Mississippi, by Smith Coffee Daniel II. The house survived the war but was destroyed by fire in 1890. Overleaf: Natchez, Mississippi combines a matchless setting and an architectural heritage that transports visitors to the romantic era of the mid-nineteenth century. Monmouth, built before 1820 was once the home of General John Anthony Quitman, hero of the Mexican War.*

This page, clockwise from left: *The sweeping staircase is one of the prize features of Monmouth. The gardens and colonnades are artfully designed to catch every cooling breeze. Visitors to Monmouth, which now serves as an exclusive inn, are greeted in the impressive front hallway where seasonal flowers are always part of the welcome. Opposite: The authentic antiques at Monmouth are so carefully mingled with reproductions that the entire setting reflects a single moment in time.*

Preceding page: *The ornate exterior of Stanton Hall, the Natchez High Street mansion built in the 1850's, is complemented by the still-gleaming chandeliers and marble mantels of the interior. This page, above: The construction of Longwood, another Natchez gem, was interrupted by the Civil War, and the interior of the unusual octagonal home was never completed. Below: Dunleith, the Natchez showplace of cotton baron Charles G. Dalhgren, was one of the most visited homes in town and is furnished with stunning French and English antiques.*

Preceding pages: *Farther west, the mansions had a French flavor. Oak Alley, on the Mississippi River west of New Orleans, is a prototypical Greek-Creole blend, created in the late 1830's by planter Jacques Telesphore Roman.* This page, clockwise from left: *A nineteenth-century four-poster bed dominates a room at Nottoway, the focal point for John Randolph's 7,000-acre sugar plantation. Containing 64 rooms, it was the largest mansion in the Old South. Despite the French heritage of Louisiana, architect Henry Howard turned to Italian villas for his inspiration for Nottoway. Today, Nottoway is an inn and restaurant.* Opposite: *Closer to New Orleans, San Francisco was another star of the antebellum sugar plantations, extravagantly decorated in Victoriana.*

Famous Southerners

The history of the Old South may have been determined by the great tides of social and intellectual forces, by the climate of the New World, and the clashes of the Old. But the particular ways those dominating factors manifested themselves were shaped by thousands and thousands of individuals, some of international importance and some of purely local fame, who captured the spirit of their age and place and through their words or deeds became the leaders.

The fire of Nathaniel Bacon, gathering freedom-loving settlers to march on Jamestown in 1676 to rebuff the authority of the British governor, first made clear that this was to be a land of independents. Exactly one hundred years later, it was the determination of another Virginian, Richard Henry Lee, that forced the colonial representatives gathered in Philadelphia to make the final break with the British Crown. It was the conviction of David Christy in his persuasive book *Cotton is King* (1855) that encouraged the South to hold tight to its economic and social policies even if it meant civil war.

The South has paid homage to its leaders by keeping intact their homes and the public buildings associated with their lives, so today we can get a glimpse of the domestic settings in which their philosophies were formed and their deeds performed. Visit the preserved homes of James Monroe, William Henry Harrison, John Tyler, and Andrew Johnson and the Presidents come alive.

The Crockett Tavern in Morrison, Tennessee, reconstructed from hand-hewn logs, helps one understand not only the simplicity of life on the frontier in the late eighteenth century but also the way in which travelers who stayed there overnight and ate with the family could have given Davy the wider breadth of vision that carried him to Washington and national fame as the "Coonskin Congressman."

Built only a few years later, but significantly grander with its two-tiered porches, Oakley House near St. Francisville, Louisiana, is a shrine to a different kind of pioneer: John James Audubon. It was here, while tutoring the daughter of the wealthy Pirrie family, that he tapped into the lush natural life of the South to find and sketch many of the species that would later be featured in his great *Birds of America*.

The men and women who have inspired and led the South have been more than regional heroes, they have been central contributors to the shaping of the entire nation. If, among so many who have played key roles, five can be spotlighted as the most influential, perhaps they are George Washington, Thomas Jefferson, Andrew Jackson, Jefferson Davis, and Robert E. Lee. They led interconnected lives: Washington and Jefferson both frequently visited beautiful Gunston Hall, the home of their friend George Mason; Jackson got his start in politics through the patronage of William Blount, the man Washington appointed as territorial governor of Tennessee; Lee and Washington were both pewholders at Christ Church in Alexandria and Lee married Martha Washington's great-granddaughter. Such connections are important in the history of the Old South.

George Washington

If any one person may be deemed the indispensable man in the creation of this country, it is George Washington. When he died at age 67 in December, 1799, Henry ("Light-Horse Harry") Lee presented to the House of Representatives a memorial resolution that acknowledged the Virginia planter to be "first in war, first in peace, and first in the hearts of his countrymen," and the phrase has lived on because it is so apt.

Unique though his particular personal combination of qualities was, he was also the quintessential product of his time and place. It was the Virginia Tidewater plantations that produced so many of America's eighteenth-century leaders exactly because their life was so balanced—between intellectual pursuits and action, between the trade of the North and the agricultural economy of the South, between an appreciation of the refinements of Europe and a love of the vigor of the American frontier—that they could conceive of a national future in continental terms.

So beloved was Washington during his life and in the developing years of the United States after his death that places even incidentally associated with him have become shrines. St. Michael's Episcopal Church in Charleston still shows visitors the pew where Washington worshipped during a 1791 visit and the steeple that he climbed to get a panoramic view of the city. Tryon Palace in New Bern, North Carolina, is another architectural gem proud of the fact that Washington stopped there on that same triumphal tour of the South. Gadsby's Tavern in Alexandria, Virginia, near Mount Vernon, is now a museum largely on the strength of the fact that Washington used to frequent it.

Washington served his nation in a staggering variety of roles. The scion of mid-seventeenth century aristocratic English émigrés, he was born in the northern neck of Virginia at Popes Creek Plantation in a house now reproduced with authentic old brick. He was appointed to his first public position—county surveyor of Culpeper County, Virginia—at the age of 17. Stafford County, Virginia, has recently acquired the land that made up Ferry Farm, Washington's boyhood home across the Rappahannock from Fredericksburg, and will reconstruct on the original foundations the buildings that were there in the eighteenth century, including the shed where the future president taught himself the art of surveying.

Before reaching the age of 25, Washington had served as district adjutant in two regions of Virginia, led colonial troops on an expedition almost to the shores of Lake Erie, seen his account of that journey become a best-selling book in both Britain and the colonies, staked out what is now Pittsburgh as a site for British fortifications, been an aide to General Braddock, commanded the forces charged with defending 300 miles of mountainous Virginia frontier against the Indians, been promoted to the rank of brigadier, taken over his half-brother's plantation, and married the widowed mother of two, Martha Dandridge Custis.

At 25, ready to trade in his youthful adventures for the life of a gentleman farmer, Washington took a seat in the House of Burgesses, charged with making his estate prosper, with seeing to the well-being of his neighbors, and with patronizing the theater and musicians. He added to the holdings of Mount Vernon and experimented with the latest in agricultural technology. Believing that mules were particularly well suited to plowing and hauling in the mountainous west, he imported jackasses from Europe and sent them on tours of what is now Kentucky to breed with mares.

And he assumed a patriarchal role in his extended family. In 1772 he built the house, still welcoming guests, in Fredericksburg, Virginia, where his mother lived for the last 17 years of her life. Fredericksburg was chosen because that was also the home of Washington's sister Betty, whose magnificent Kenmore, with its decorative molded plaster ceilings, still awes visitors. George Washington's youngest brother, Charles, also lived in Fredericksburg, and the Rising Sun Tavern he ran has been restored to the way it looked in 1760 when it was a major stagecoach stop.

But Washington's innate talent for national leadership was clear, and he would not refuse a call to serve the public. He acted as agent for his former troops in procuring for them western land they had been promised as pay for their military service. He led the opposition to the increasingly onerous British taxation policy toward the colonies, declaring that Parliament "hath no more right to put their hands into my pocket without my consent than I have to put my hands into yours for money." He was a Virginia delegate to the First Continental Congress in 1774 and to the Second Continental Congress the following year.

By then war with Britain clearly loomed over the colonies, and the Continental Congress realized that some sort of unified military force was going to be necessary. But unification was still a fragile concept among the colonies, with northern settlements and those in the South suspicious of each other and committed to different goals. The one man they could all agree on to head the troops from North and South was Washington. His one stipulation before accepting the command: that he would receive no pay for the position.

Washington was more than a commander who could hold together the regional factions, of course: he proved to be a brilliant tactician and an inspiring leader. His defense of New York in 1776 against overwhelming British forces and his night retreat that avoided a military disaster is still studied as a classic maneuver. Later that year, with his Christmas night crossing of the Delaware and capture of the Trenton fort manned by Hessians, he served notice to the British that the colonials would not be an easy foe. In battle after battle, he deployed the forces of the fledgling nation like those of an established power, culminating in the surrender of Cornwallis at Yorktown.

Again Washington attempted to return to the life of a country squire and to tend to badly needed improvements at Mount Vernon. And again national duty called: he agreed to chair the convention called to develop a constitution to replace the increasingly ineffective Articles of Confederation. When that constitution was adopted by the states, he turned aside suggestions that he should take the role of president of the new nation, insisting that he had no "wish beyond that of living and dying an honest man on my own farm."

How different the history of the nation might have been had he clung to that wish for a totally private life. Finally acceding to the demands that only he could provide a leadership that all 13 states would respect, he provided exactly the pragmatic direction the country needed. Dismissing the philosophical debates on the nature of man and the proper role of government that were so common in the eighteenth century, he saw to it that the United States got on with the business of setting up a government: establishing courts, building roads, raising an army, and developing foreign relationships that would allow the nation decades of peace in which to get itself on a firm footing. He carefully balanced his cabinet between liberals and conservatives, insisting that the government as a whole should be above party factions. Visit William Blount's mansion in Knoxville, Tennessee, to see how Washington, by appointing Blount governor of the territory, ensured the westward expansion of the United States.

After two terms, he retired to Mount Vernon, still viewing with modesty his accomplishments and talents. "Though in reviewing the incidents of my administration I am unconscious of intentional error, I am nevertheless too sensible of my defects not to think it probable that I may have committed many errors," he said in his farewell address. "I shall carry with me the hope that my country will never cease to view them with indulgence, and that, after 45 years of my life dedicated to its service with an upright zeal, the faults of incompetent abilities will be consigned to oblivion, as myself must soon be to the mansions of rest."

Washington was not yet able to shed public responsibilities: once again, in 1789, he put on his general's uniform to command a provisional army gathered in case a developing conflict with France should turn into a shooting war. The nation did, finally, let Washington return to Mount Vernon, where he brought the most modern agricultural measures into play—he was one of the first planters to rotate crops to keep the land from wearing out. He watched carefully as the capital of his nation was created from swampland just down the Potomac from his plantation. He divided 2,038 acres of his estate and gave them as a wedding present to his wife's granddaughter Nelly when she married Washington's nephew, Lawrence Lewis, and then he commissioned William Thornton to design the mansion that is still the focal point of Woodlawn Plantation. Thornton, a Scottish physician, was such a successful amateur architect that he won the competition to design the Capitol.

Washington remained a folk hero. During his lifetime, his birthday was celebrated with dances and other festivities. Wherever he went, troops paraded and streets were festooned. Just weeks before his death, George and Martha Washington were asked to take part in the Winter Assemblies in Alexandria. He answered: "Thank you for this mark of attention. But alas! our dancing days are no more." Washington had the "decade of domestic felicity" he so wished for.

THOMAS JEFFERSON

When Washington assumed the Presidency of the United States, he turned to Thomas Jefferson to fill the senior cabinet position— the job of Secretary of State. Not yet 50, Jefferson had already accumulated a wealth of experience in foreign affairs that made him a logical choice for the job. But his diplomatic accomplishments were only one aspect of this truly Renaissance man, the possessor of both deep intelligence and a wide breadth of interests and talents.

John F. Kennedy summed up well the modern view of the nation's third President when, at a 1962 dinner for American winners of the Nobel Prize, he said, "I think this is the most extraordinary collection of talent, of human knowledge, that has ever been gathered together at the White House—with the possible exception of when Thomas Jefferson dined alone."

Jefferson was born into an orbit of standing and prestige because his mother was a Randolph, one of the highest-ranked of the First Families of Virginia, although his father, a surveyor and landowner, was only modestly wealthy. Jefferson spent much of his boyhood at Tuckahoe, the plantation of his mother's cousin William Randolph, still an elegantly preserved private family home and working farm. "Not only is the house priceless because of its completeness, but it contains some of the most important architectural ideas of the early Georgian period," University of Virginia historian Frederick Nichols wrote in his book about the property. "Probably unique in American architecture are the rare outbuildings, including paired structures which were the office and schoolhouse where Thomas Jefferson went to classes."

He was a frequent visitor, too, at Carter's Grove, the elegant Georgian mansion overlooking the James River near Williamsburg. The impact of living amid such architectural splendor clearly influenced the young Jefferson, and provided one thread of interest for him to pursue when he enrolled in the College of William and Mary in 1760. But he absorbed a boggling array of other subjects there too, from the latest eighteenth-century scientific discoveries to the philosophy of John Locke to the fine points of law.

Admitted to the bar in 1767, he built a successful practice and began to put together the life of a Virginia squire. He became a member of the House of Burgesses in 1769, and the next year began construction of Monticello, his house near Charlottesville on which he would work for most of the rest of his life, converting over the years what had begun as a modest home into a 21-room classic, the first house in America with a dome. In 1772, he married Martha Wayles Skelton.

But Locke had left his mark on Jefferson, who mated his establishment life to a radical political belief that interpreted the laws of nature as guaranteeing man's right to freedom. "A little rebellion now and then is a good thing," he once noted in a letter to his ally and neighbor, James Madison. Jefferson acknowledged the sovereignty of King George III, but insisted that was the end of the American colonies' tie with Britain—that Parliament had no authority to write rules governing those on the western shore of the Atlantic nor to impose taxes on them. Jefferson knew that he was not an effective public debater, and that his natural skill in writing was the route to win people's hearts and minds. He helped create the Virginia Committee of Correspondence to promulgate those views, and he set them forth formally in *A Summary View of the Rights of British America* in 1774.

Virginia sent him as a delegate to the Philadelphia meeting where his fellow Virginian, Richard Henry Lee, called for a declaration of independence from Britain. Given the passion and logic of his previous writings, it was fitting that the convention turned to Jefferson to write what was adopted as the Declaration of Independence. It is still not only the finest embodiment of the American dream, but also a clarion call to freedom that has inspired people around the globe. A long string of major accomplishments were ahead for Jefferson and the tyro nation, but no other achievement summed up his zeal so well as his authorship of the Declaration.

While Washington was masterminding the military victory over the British, Jefferson was working to create a model for the democratic nation that was to emerge from the war. In the Virginia legislature and as governor, he led the fight to abolish the trappings of the aristocracy, championing such causes as religious freedom and the abolition of entails and primogeniture, so that massive land holdings would be broken up into smaller estates rather than automatically passing intact to the first-born son.

After the Revolutionary War had been won, Jefferson paid more attention to private life, bringing modern agricultural methods to the operation of Monticello and writing optimistic descriptions of the New World that gained him fame in the Old. He was one of the first to employ contour plowing, with furrows following the lay of the land, and, like Washington, to rotate his crops. He experimented with more than 250 varieties of fruits, vegetables, and herbs.

But at the same time, Jefferson continued to accept public roles: as a member of the Congress convened under the Articles of Confederation; as a member of the U.S. delegation negotiating commercial treaties with various European nations; and as minister to France, where he noted in detail the development of the French Revolution. He was heartened by the way his own Declaration of Independence became a rallying cry for others but also by the way his nation had moved toward democracy without the civic violence he saw in France.

Foreign service, of course, prepared him for Washington's call to serve as Secretary of State. He helped mold the neutrality of the new nation toward the conflagrations sweeping Europe, but he was locked in constant battle with Treasury Secretary Alexander Hamilton over what Jefferson saw as Hamilton's antidemocratic efforts to expand the authority of the executive into matters the Constitution had

left up to Congress. Wearying of the controversy, Jefferson in 1794 retired to Monticello, but accepted the position of Vice-President under John Adams "to put our vessel on her republican tack before she should be thrown too much to leeward of her true principles."

His writings, however, made him the foremost voice in the United States for the developing liberal political tradition—the side that put the greater faith in the wisdom of the people. Jefferson and Aaron Burr received identical electoral vote totals in the 1800 election, but the House of Representatives picked Jefferson. It was typical of the close-knit Virginia aristocracy that he was sworn into the Presidency by his cousin, John Marshall, already serving as Chief Justice of the United States.

Returning again to Monticello in 1809, Jefferson devoted much of the rest of his life to putting a physical imprint on his nation. "Architecture is my delight, and putting up and pulling down one of my favorite amusements," he once wrote. He had already designed the Virginia State Capitol in Richmond. After his Presidency, Jefferson founded the University of Virginia and designed its original campus, just down the mountain from Monticello. The serpentine wall with which he surrounded the original campus—an undulating row of red bricks—still delights visitors today. He continued to build his plantation house into perhaps the finest example of the Federal-period country home. And he designed for friends and relatives houses that we still cherish, including Highland, Madison's home just up the road from Monticello, now called Ash Lawn, which, though gracious, bespeaks a life less opulent than that lived at Monticello.

And he wrote. Twelve miles from Lynchburg, Virginia, he built Poplar Forest, a modest octagonal one-story house he used as a personal retreat from Monticello, where he continued to face the demands of public life. At Poplar Forest, he showed himself an inexhaustibly energetic correspondent, pouring out a flow of letters inspiring colleagues in Europe and the United States to continue the fight for liberty. His fertile mind kept developing gadgets, now on display at Monticello, to make life easier. Primary among them are those related to his letter-writing: a revolving table and a "polygraph" which wrote a copy of a letter as Jefferson penned the original. Of greater interest perhaps is his correspondence with the man he served as Vice-President, John Adams, and it seems fitting that both died the same day, July 4, 1826, the fiftieth anniversary of the Declaration of Independence.

ANDREW JACKSON

Washington and Jefferson were typical of the first generation of American leaders: aristocratic, landowning, raised near the Atlantic shores where Europeans first settled in the New World. Andrew Jackson's unique place in history is that he was the first national leader to emerge from another tradition: he was the first son of the frontier to occupy the White House. If Jefferson has come to stand for the intellectual belief that a society is best ruled by its own inhabitants, Jackson personifies a down-and-dirty appreciation for the common man with all his untutored ways and basic common sense.

Born in 1767 in Waxhaw Settlement in South Carolina, Jackson's early life was not one of privilege. His father had died before Jackson was born, and before Jackson was 15 his mother and two brothers also had died. While a prisoner of the British, after being captured at the Revolutionary War battle of Hanging Rock, he contracted smallpox. Full of a youthful zest for adventure, he found his way to the new log cabin town of Nashville (in what was then part of North Carolina), where he parlayed a desultory study of the law into an appointment as local prosecutor and began courting the divorced daughter of his landlady. Andrew Jackson and Rachel Robards were married in 1791 at Springfield, a still-standing plantation house near Tupelo, Mississippi.

As the territory developed and finally pulled away as a separate state, Jackson's circle of experience widened. He was a delegate to the convention that drafted the Tennessee constitution, was elected to the House of Representatives once Tennessee was admitted to the Union, and at the age of 30 became his adopted state's United States Senator. Tiring of life in Washington, he resigned his seat to return to Tennessee, where he and Rachel lived in a log house on a tract of land 12 miles east of Nashville. He prospered as a cotton grower there and held a variety of public offices.

It was the War of 1812 that set his destiny, for he was put in charge of the Tennessee militia and his personal daring and innate ability to command turned him into both an effective military leader and a charismatic popular hero. Much of his fighting was against the Creek Indians, who were allied with the British. Early in the conflict, he defeated the Creeks at Talladega, Alabama and rescued a trapped group of townspeople.

But the mythic legend was forged at Horseshoe Bend in the Tallapoosa River near where Dadeville, Alabama, is now. Visitors to the national military park there can view the site of Jackson's victory over the Creek Indians, who had barricaded themselves behind the narrowest part of the peninsula made by the river's turning back on itself. A consequence of this victory was that the United States gained title to land that makes up 60 percent of Georgia and about 20 percent of Alabama.

But if it was Horseshoe Bend that garnered Jackson national attention, it was the Battle of New Orleans at Christmastime, 1814, that turned him into an unstoppable political force. Although Britain and the United States had already signed the treaty ending the war, the news was slow to reach New Orleans. Sir Edward Pakenham advanced on the city with 10,000 experienced troops, twice as many as Jackson could muster to defend it even with his militia augmented by raw recruits. At a place that would later be the site of the U.S. Mint, Jackson reviewed his troops and sent them into the fray. With a combination of wise tactics and inspiring determination, Jackson held the line against assault after assault, finally wreaking such devastation on the British troops that Pakenham surrendered. The naming of the central square in New Orleans for Jackson is only one indication of the adulation that Jackson received for the victory.

One historian writes of Jackson at this juncture of his career: "Tall, slender, narrowfaced, friend to friends and implacable to enemies, he was able, when he chose, to restrain his high temper or play it up for the sake of effect. Although he denied he sought office, it was clear that he was a presidential possibility." Locations even casually touched by Jackson became shrines: at Sandy Hook, Mississippi, for instance, the home of John Ford, a Methodist minister, became a tourist destination because Ford put Jackson up for the night on his way to New Orleans.

The log home back in Tennessee no longer seemed appropriate for that kind of hero. So Rachel Jackson selected a site on a 625-acre plantation overlooking the rolling countryside where the couple built the grand house known as The Hermitage. It contains an elegant curved stairway rising from the front hall and a carved mantelpiece commemorating the victory at New Orleans.

Jackson became even more of a national hero later in the decade, when he led the troops that invaded Florida and won the peninsula, still Spanish territory, for the United States. He became its first territorial governor, with headquarters in Pensacola in the northern panhandle. The ruins of Fort Gadsden, fortified under Jackson's orders as a supply depot for the Spanish campaign, are now preserved as a Florida historical site.

Jackson was clearly a man who had the popular touch. He produced almost a frenzy of support among frontiersmen and ordinary citizens who were for the first time becoming important in determining the outcome of national elections. They backed him not because of his political philosophy—which was generally more conservative than that of his supporters—but because of personal loyalty. In Jackson they saw the common man magnified.

In fact, Jackson's lack of identification with a clear set of national policies became an asset: it was perceived as independence, a quality much admired in the new western reaches of the nation. He was popular enough to garner the most votes of any candidate in the 1824 Presidential election, but with no one having a majority in the electoral college, John Quincy Adams won the post in the House of Representatives. Jackson's backers— especially the followers of W. H. Crawford in Georgia and Virginia—were outraged and worked for four years to avenge the loss. In the next election, they carried "Old Hickory" to the White House.

The period was marked by personal tragedy for Jackson. Rachel died shortly before his inauguration. The Hermitage was gutted by fire midway through his second term.

Nonetheless, Jackson's presidency is rated one of the most successful in American history, an era when populist policies diminished the power of the bankers, when U.S. trading relationships with the British holdings in the West Indies were regularized, when much of the land west of the Mississippi was made safe for settlement. The tone of the administration was set immediately, as Jackson threw open the doors of the White House to the hoards of well-wishers who had come to Washington to see his inauguration. The boisterous party that followed owed virtually nothing to the genteel protocols established by Jackson's six predecessors in the highest office in the land, but made eminently clear that America was to be a country ruled by the people. A dismayed Justice Joseph Story commented about the party, "I was glad to escape from the scene as soon as possible."

Jackson's political decisions were pragmatic responses to individual developments, without an overriding political philosophy. But his rhetoric tapped the right response cords in his populist supporters, as when he wrote: "There are no necessary evils in government. Its evils exist only in its abuses. If it would confine itself to equal protection, and, as Heaven does its rains, shower its favors alike on the high and the low, the rich and the poor, it would be an unqualified blessing."

But the southerner did not seem at the time to be always a staunch supporter of the South. Starting his first term with John C. Calhoun, the very personification of the South's belief in states' rights, as Vice-President, Jackson dumped him in his second term to pave the way for Martin Van Buren to be his successor. Jackson came down hard on South Carolina when the state threatened secession over the steep tariffs enacted on the eve of Jackson's election.

But the President ended his term as much a national hero as he was when he started it. He rebuilt The Hermitage, grander than before, adding the two-story galleries and facade of fluted columns that today are the most vivid impression visitors carry away from the shrine. On a corner of the estate he built Tulip Grove, also still intact, as a home for his nephew and namesake, who had served as his private secretary in the White House and continued as his aide in his final years. Jackson had eight years more to enjoy the adulation of the populace and the peace of his plantation.

JEFFERSON DAVIS

A century and a quarter after the Civil War, the phrases

"states' rights" and "the Confederacy" seem to pair neatly. But in the middle of the nineteenth century they were in many ways opposing concepts: some of the staunchest secessionists—politicians like Robert Barnwell Rhett of South Carolina, William Lowndes Yancey of Alabama, and John A. Quitman of Mississippi—took the states' rights concept to its ultimate conclusion and argued that the individual southern states should act on their own. The leading spokesman for the other point of view was Jefferson Davis; he never wavered in his loyalty to the entire South nor in his belief that regional solidarity was essential.

How appropriate that Davis should have been selected to head the government of the Confederate States of America! That was not the job Davis wanted. By the time the southern states met in Montgomery in the first weeks of 1861 to form the secessionist government, Davis had compiled a resumé of regional and national leadership impressive in its scope. But his own greatest enthusiasm—and his own view of his abilities—centered on the military. He had hoped to win the job of commander-in-chief of the Confederate army.

Raised at Rosemont Plantation in Mississippi (still maintained for the public as a working plantation) Davis went on to Jefferson College in Washington, Mississippi. He transferred to the U.S. Military Academy at West Point and graduated in 1828, a year ahead of Robert E. Lee. A tragic love, however, cut his military career short. As a young commissioned officer he served at frontier posts in Illinois and Wisconsin, where, at Fort Crawford, he fell in love with the daughter of his commanding officer, the future U.S. President Zachary Taylor. Although Colonel Taylor opposed the match, Sarah Taylor and Davis nonetheless got married, but at the same time Davis resigned from the Army. A bare three months later, Sarah died.

Over the next decade, Davis built a new life for himself. His parents' tenth child, Jefferson Davis had always looked to his eldest brother Joseph for guidance, almost as a surrogate father. Davis settled at Brierfield, a Mississippi plantation adjacent to Joseph's, and, under his tutelage, read voraciously and became a successful landowner. In 1845 he married Varina Howell and won a seat in Congress.

But then America found itself again at war, and Davis put his military training first. He resigned as a lawmaker and took command of a volunteer regiment in the Mexican War. His troops' brave stand at the battle of Buena Vista turned a likely defeat into victory, and on the crest of that success Davis resigned his commission and was selected U.S. Senator from Mississippi.

In that forum, he became a voice of the southern nationalists, arguing against the 1850 compromise as giving the South too little, and against the secessionists who wanted each state to go its own way. In 1851, he left the Senate to run for governor of Mississippi and was defeated. Two years later, he was back in Washington as Franklin Pierce's Secretary of War, where he was an ardent advocate of southern expansion. He was instrumental in the U.S. making the Gadsden Purchase of land along the Mexican border to provide a corridor for a railway from the South to the Pacific.

He went back to the Senate in 1857, furiously working behind the scenes for a compromise that would let the South follow its own destiny without a complete break with the Union, perhaps through some sort of dominion status. But when the splitting of the nation became inevitable, he reluctantly took the helm of the Confederacy. When he was inaugurated, orator Robert Toombs commented: "The man and the hour have met."

Davis insisted that the entire philosophical reason for the split was to allow the South to develop according to its own standards. He summed it up in his first address to the Confederate Congress: "All we ask is to be let alone." The bold vision of those would-be framers of a new nation can still be felt in visits to the Alabama State Capitol in Montgomery, where the government was forged, and to the first White House of the Confederacy, where portraits of the Davis family dominate the displays of Confederate artifacts.

Moving from Montgomery to Richmond, Davis spent his efforts trying—largely unsuccessfully—to win support in Europe for the self-proclaimed nation; one of his first acts as President of the Confederacy was to impose an embargo on cotton exports, but it did not have the desired effect of making Britain and France recognize the Confederacy as an independent state. Documentation of these diplomatic struggles is now held in the Museum of the Confederacy in Richmond, next door to the Clay Street home that served as the Presidential Mansion while Davis lived in Richmond.

The main task for Davis there was to hold the alliance together in the face of the growing political power of the states' righters. In fact, in the Confederate Congress elections of 1863, the voters returned a majority opposed to the curbs Davis wanted to put on the sovereignty of the individual member states.

It was his fierce devotion to the idea of unity that held the Confederacy together. He chose the most able officers to lead the troops, regardless of their state of origin, even though many Confederate governors argued that only native sons should command each state's militia. He insisted on giving the military the manpower it needed, even though the conscription law he rammed through the legislature was generally unpopular. And Davis maintained the social role of a head of state, staging glittering parties at the gray stucco Presidential Mansion known as the White House of the Confederacy.

But that house of happiness became for Davis a shrine of sadness in 1864 when his young son was killed in a fall from the porch. The tragedy seemed symbolic, for by then the fighting had worsened for the Confederacy; Davis used his presidential power to revoke the exemptions from the draft that had been ordered, even calling back to arms those furloughed and hospitalized soldiers who were still able to fight. At the time, Davis declared, "Two-thirds of our men are absent, most of them without leave."

By early 1865, Davis's representatives and those of Lincoln had worked out a compromise to end the hostilities, but Davis refused to accept it because he insisted on independence for the South—something that Washington would never accede to. He held on. When Richmond was about to fall, Davis moved the government to Danville, Virginia. When Lee surrendered, he moved the government again, this time to Charlotte, North Carolina. He fled south from there, and was finally captured by Union troops at Irwinville, Georgia.

In a way, Davis never gave up. Denied the popular adulation that cushioned Lee's post-Civil War years, Davis remained the voice of a united South. In 1877, he came for an extended stay with an old friend, Sara Dorsey, at the cottage called Beauvoir not far from Biloxi, and so fell in love with the floor-to-ceiling windows that caught every breeze off the Gulf that he bought the house and land. There he worked 15 years on his *Rise and Fall of the Confederate Government,* which for generations of southerners was the official history of those brave and disastrous five years. Eight years after it was published in 1881, Davis died in New Orleans.

Beauvoir was converted into a home for Confederate veterans, but today serves as a shrine to the sole President of the Confederacy. His desk is displayed in the library pavilion where he wrote his history, and memorabilia from his long political career are preserved. Also on the grounds, fittingly enough, is the Tomb of the Unknown Soldier of the Confederate States of America.

Had the final break between the South and the Union never come, the achievements of Robert E. Lee would still have won him a secure place in the pantheon of American heroes. The brilliance, dynamism, and compassion he displayed as commander-in-chief of the Confederate troops had already been evident in his military service to his country.

Six days after the first shots were fired at Fort Sumter, Lincoln asked Lee to become field commander of the Union Army. Lee had opposed secession but had vowed he would never battle his home state. On April 20, when Virginia joined the Confederacy, Lee resigned from the Union Army and totally committed his passion and energies to the Southern cause.

It is no wonder that each side wanted Lee as a leader, for he had proved his outstanding abilities in post after post, displaying a nobility and gentility not often consonant with military success. He was second in his class at West Point. In 1837, at the age of 30, he was put in charge of the river and harbor construction work at St. Louis and did an admirable job. In the Mexican War, he played a key role in virtually every battle from Vera Cruz to Chapultepec. He was rewarded with the superintendency of West Point.

In 1855, Lee was promoted to lieutenant colonel and put back in charge of troops: the Second Cavalry. In that position he led the soldiers who captured the abolitionist John Brown after the attack on the arsenal at Harper's Ferry in 1859.

Lee's distinction was that he was always more than a soldier. He had charm and courtliness and an in-bred dedication to public service. His father, popularly known as Light-Horse Harry Lee, had been one of George Washington's most esteemed subordinates in the Revolutionary War but had never seemed contented in civilian life. From an early age Robert was determined not to let the military set the boundaries of his existence. As the master of Arlington House, Washington's wedding gift to his wife's grandparents, he was at the center of the social whirl where so many of the standards of the Old South were preserved and passed on.

To be a Lee in Virginia was a great privilege, but also a great responsibility. In the mid-seventeenth century, Richard Lee had founded the dynasty in Virginia. By the time Robert E. Lee was born in 1807, not only had his father made a major contribution to the military victory of the Revolutionary War, but four of his father's cousins were also instrumental in the political battles that created the new nation: Richard Henry Lee, who goaded the Continental Congress into declaring independence from Britain; Francis Lightfoot Lee, another signer of the Declaration of Independence; Arthur Lee, the emissary of the Continental Congress to France; and William Lee, the fledgling nation's representative to Austria, Prussia, and the Netherlands.

Evidence of the Lees' life in Virginia abounds today. Perhaps the most important site is Stratford Hall, the plantation house near Lerty, Virginia. An unusual H-shaped mansion built in the 1730's of brick made on the site and timber cut from the property's forests, it spreads out from a great square central hall which measures 29 feet on each side. From this command post a major plantation was run, producing not only tobacco but also wheat, oats, and barley—which were ground in Stratford's own mill—as well as garden vegetables and apples for the famous Stratford cider. But family affairs were run from there too; built by Thomas Lee, colonial governor of Virginia, Stratford Hall not only was the home of his famous sons but also the meeting point for the entire extended family. It was here that Robert E. Lee was born.

Sully Plantation in Chantilly, Virginia, now a historic property of the Fairfax County Park Authority, was the home built by Richard Bland Lee (Light-Horse Harry's brother and northern Virginia's first selection to serve in the House of Representatives) on land bought by his grandfather, Henry Lee, in 1725. Leesburg, Virginia, is named for Francis Lightfoot, who owned land near there.

A visit today to the town of Alexandria will show how embedded the Lee family was in the fabric of that historic village. Robert's father's home on Cameron Street is still in use as a private residence. Less than five blocks away is the home where Lee spent his boyhood, a house where Washington and Lafayette visited and which today preserves the essence of the southern Federal period. Between the two is Fendall House, built in 1785 by Robert Fendall, a friend of Washington's and Light-Horse Harry Lee's, and later a home to various members of the Lee clan for more than a century. It is ideal to visit in late January; Robert E. Lee was born on January 21 and his father on January 29, and to celebrate the two birthdays visitors around those dates are treated to period musicales and appropriate refreshments.

It is no wonder that once the Civil War had begun, Lee rallied to the South's cause. Although immediately named commander of the Virginia forces, Lee was always committed to a unified view of the Confederacy, serving as the military consultant to President Jefferson Davis and insisting that the troops of the individual states of the Confederacy be treated as a single military force.

He organized the defense of the southern Atlantic coast against invasion from Union ships. Taking over field command from wounded General Joseph E. Johnston in June of 1862, he turned back advancing Union forces which had reached to within seven miles of the capital at Richmond. He turned a defensive posture into an aggressive one, pushing the opposing army almost 100 miles back to Washington.

The victory gave Lee a reputation of being able to overcome great disadvantages in number, of planning strategy and inspiring soldiers so that they could best twice or three times their numbers. With able assistance from Stonewall Jackson—who as Lee's executive officer had an uncanny ability to translate Lee's plans into action—Lee routed the Union troops under General John Pope at the second battle of Bull Run on August 30, 1862.

From there he invaded Union territory in Maryland. Over the next year, brilliant victories followed, especially those at Fredericksburg and Chancellorsville. But ultimately, of course, Lee was unable to resist the superior Union resources, and after the defeat at Gettysburg the outcome of the war seemed inevitable. He built effective field fortifications and had a sixth sense for when the Union Army would strike next and how to outmaneuver the enemy, but the talent merely allowed the Confederacy to hold on longer. At the Battle of Sailor's Creek, Lee lost 8,000 men and knew that the end was at hand. To drive the auto route through the battlefield near Green Bay, Virginia, is to reexperience the despair of that fateful day. Three days later, Lee surrendered at Appomattox and moved into a house in Richmond that today looks much as it did in 1865, through it is now a popular downtown restaurant.

Lee did not stay long in Richmond. By autumn, he had moved to Lexington, Virginia, to take up his new challenge: the presidency of Washington College, a training ground for the sons of established southern families which had been devastated by the war. As president of the institution, he worked tirelessly for the final five years of his life to restore it to its former excellence. Fittingly, he first lived in the house where his former executive officer once had lived, for Stonewall Jackson, 19 years earlier, had married the daughter of one of Lee's predecessors as president of Washington College. Lee eventually designed another house to serve as the official residence on campus, and lived there from 1868 until his death in 1870. Both houses, as well as his tomb in what is now known as Lee Chapel are preserved as tributes to the Confederate general, for whom the college renamed itself Washington & Lee.

The post of college president provided Robert E. Lee an opportunity beyond Lexington; it was a platform from which to preach a message of healing and rebuilding. Lee's reputation reached a zenith in the postwar years. Frank Buscher, a Swiss portraitist who traveled through the States between 1865 and 1870 painting the celebrated, commented that Lee was the only great man he met in his journeys. Buscher's portrait of Lee, now in the Kunstmuseum in Berne, shows him in mufti, his Confederate uniform folded at his side and his sword sheathed, a leader in peacetime as he was in war.

Lee urged the South to put the enmity of secession behind it, to restore its economy and its cultural life, to play again its unique role in making the entire United States a richer, more chivalrous, more exciting nation. The modern South that prospers today is a fitting tribute to his vision.

This page: Sugar brought prosperity to the bayous west of the Mississippi, creating plantation houses there like Shadows-on-the-Teche, the headquarters for Union general William B. Franklin in the waning days of the Civil War. Opposite: In Virginia's Tidewater area, the country's tenth president, John Tyler, made his home at the elegant Sherwood Forest near Jamestown. A loyal son of the South, he became a member of the lower house of the Confederate Congress, but died in the first weeks of 1862, before the legislature met.

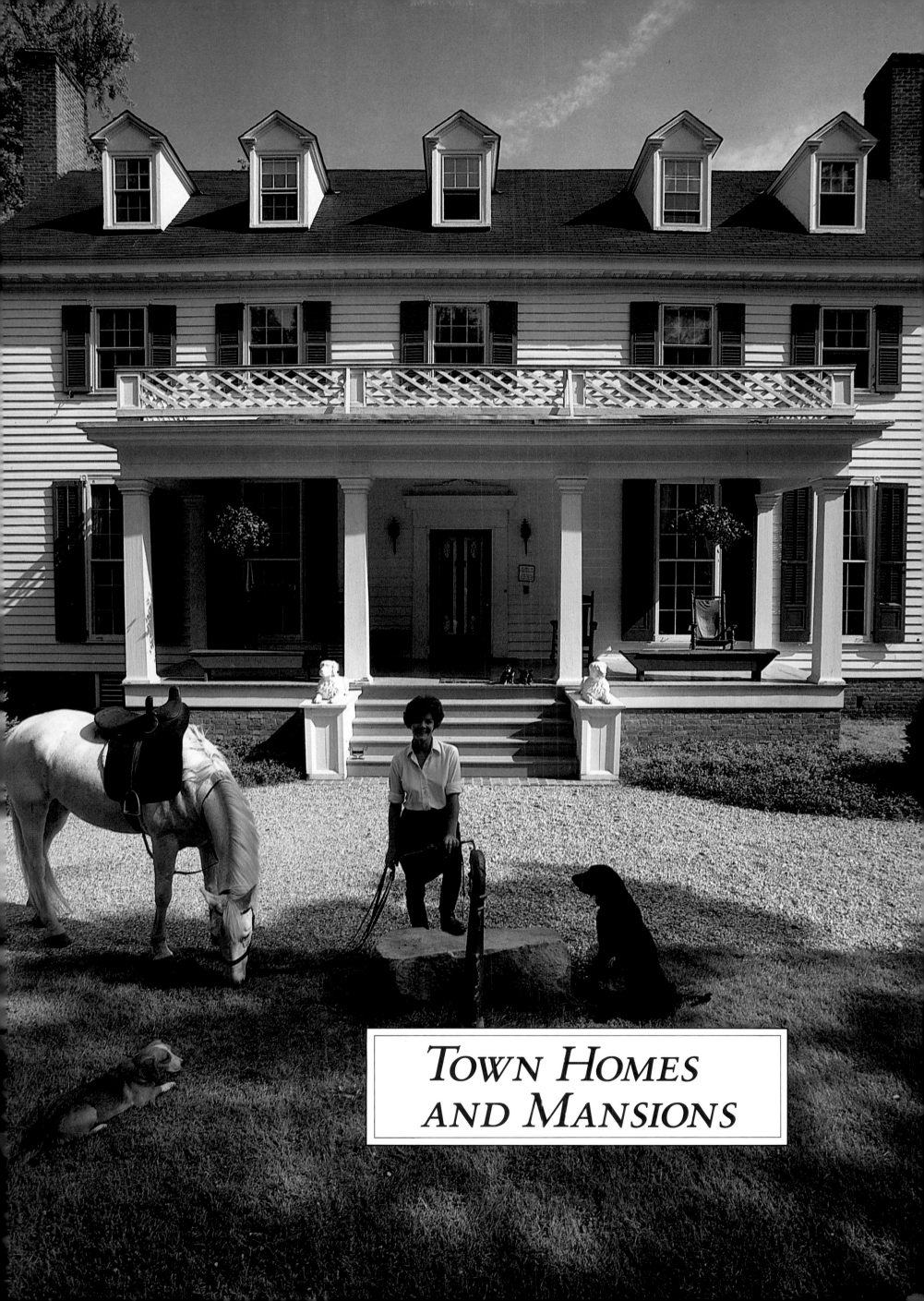

TOWN HOMES
AND MANSIONS

This page, above: *Now a gathering place for the tourists who throng to Alexandria, Virginia, Ramsay House is the oldest structure in town, built in 1724.* Below: *Just one block north of Ramsay House is Carlyle House, the scene, in 1755, of a meeting between General Edward Braddock—whom Washington served as an aide—and the British governors of five American colonies, where the strategy for the French and Indian War was planned.*

The brick-paved streets of the old section of Alexandria follow the scheme laid out in the late 1740's by surveyor John West, Jr. and his assistant, George Washington.

Preceding page: *The Cupola House in Edenton, North Carolina, incorporates Jacobean design elements common in New England but seldom found in the Old South.* This page, clockwise from left: *The eight-sided cupola which gave the house its name was used to observe arriving and departing ships. The Hezekiah Alexander house, the oldest now standing in Charlotte, North Carolina, was built in 1774. Alexander built his main dwelling of fieldstone, but the kitchen and barn were constructed of hand-hewn logs.* Following pages, left: *In their teen years, Moravian boys in Old Salem came to the Single Brothers' House to learn a trade in one of the shops; when they had moved beyond apprentice status, they moved into the dormitory on the upper floor, where they lived until they married.* Right: *Washington visited Old Salem, North Carolina, and was fascinated by the Moravians' planned community and simple, structured life.*

Preceding pages: *This kitchen restoration captures the pared-down, ordered approach to life that was the hallmark of the Moravian community in Old Salem. This page, clockwise from left: The married craftsmen used the ground floors of their homes as stores where they sold their crafts; tobacco was the main product at this shop on South Main. The shops in Old Salem feature symbolic signs, such as this one at the bootmaker's, that let illiterate customers know what was for sale. Hats were important articles of clothing in defining propriety and class in the third decade of the nineteenth century. Opposite: The beehive on this merchant's shop sign is a symbol of industriousness.*

This page, clockwise from left: *The Moravians who moved south from Pennsylvania originally built the settlement called Bethabara (Hebrew for "House of Passage"); men living there built Salem later. Only in the mid-1960's did the job of restoring Bethabara begin, with the 1788 church the first—and perhaps finest—example of the work of the preservationists. In Bethabara, the Moravians planted herbs and flowers that were unusual in the area.* Opposite: *The Nathaniel Russell House on Meeting Street in Charleston, South Carolina, is a fine example of the Adam style.*

Preceding pages: *Nathaniel Russell, a son of the Chief Justice of Rhode Island, was a wealthy merchant during the first decades of the nineteenth century; the period furnishings in his house demonstrate the opulent style typical of that class and time. This page, above: Broad Street, the site of the colonial marketplace and, later, the Bank of the U.S. and City Hall, has long been a major thoroughfare in Charleston. Below: Southerners' pride in their heritage is evidenced in the immaculate care with which the Rainbow Row residences on East Bay Street are maintained.*

This page, above: *Tourists are drawn past the Edmonston-Alston House, a Greek Revival beauty with an unspoiled view of the harbor.* Below: *The Calhoun Mansion is still furnished in the elaborate style of the mid-Victorian period and boasts exquisite gardens and a 75-foot-high glass-domed ceiling. Following page: All along Church Street — the home of the only church in the U.S. that still uses Huguenot liturgy — are mansions more than 150 years old.*

This page, above: *The oldest settlement in South Carolina, Camden served Cornwallis as the British headquarters for the entire South during the Revolutionary War.* Below: *The Joseph Manigault House is a particular delight for visitors because it actually has what so many southern mansions are falsely rumored to feature: a hidden staircase. Overleaf: On lush Reynolds Square in Savannah, Georgia, the Olde Pink House, built in 1771, is of historic importance—the state's first bank was housed here—but it is even more a gastronomic shrine: today it is a restaurant keeping alive colonial cuisine.*

This page: *The Green-Meldrim House, with distinctive ironwork verandas, served as Sherman's Savannah headquarters in 1864, 11 years after it was built.*
Opposite: *The fanciful balcony supports are typical of the ornate detailing throughout Savannah's Owens-Thomas House, architect William Jay's masterpiece in the English Regency style.*

Preceding page: *Savannah was the landing point for General James Oglethorpe when he founded the Georgia colony with 122 settlers in 1733.* This page, above: *These proud Savannah mansions are not only architectural showplaces but real family dwellings where the traditions of civility have been passed from generation to generation. Below: One of Savannah's finest residences is the Italianate home that was designed by architect John S. Norris in 1848 for the British cotton merchant Andrew Low; it was later the home of Juliette Gordon Low, the founder of the Girl Scouts.*

Preceding page: *The villa-like Hay House is one of the prides of Macon, Georgia, the bustling river town that was the home port of the Pioneer, the very first of the southern river steamers.* This page, clockwise from left: *The Italianate style that William Butler Johnson decreed for Hay House was reflected in the opulent interior decoration and furnishings. Cascades of crystal form the chandeliers in the ballroom furnishings. Johnson ordered 19 mantelpieces of Carrara marble for Hay House.* Overleaf: *The generously shaded colonnades of southern houses provided cooling relief from the summertime sun.*

The T-shaped Oakleigh plantation home, built in the mid-1830's, has given its name to a Mobile neighborhood full of fine residences.

This page: *Empire furnishings set the tone for life at Oakleigh, built on the highest point of land in the original Spanish land grant. Overleaf: Beauvoir, five miles west of Biloxi, Mississippi, was the home of Confederate president Jefferson Davis for the final 12 years of his life. After his death in 1889, it served as a home for Confederate widows and veterans until the beginning of World War II, and today the grounds provide an appropriate setting for the Tomb of the Unknown Soldier of the Confederate States.*

This page: *Adjacent to the main house at Beauvoir is the Library Pavilion, where Davis wrote the two key books that give the Confederate view of the Civil War:* The Rise and Fall of the Confederate Government *and* A Short History of the Confederate States of America. *Opposite: A portrait of Davis dominates this parlor at Beauvoir. The property was bought by Davis after being released from Fortress Monroe, where he was imprisoned at the end of the war.*

This page, above: *Perhaps the most exuberant city of the Old South is New Orleans, where "steamboat houses," designed to look like the showboats of the Mississippi River, capture the entire area's insouciant spirit.* Below: *In New Orleans' Garden District, the homes are not the dwellings of the aristocracy as they once were, but the gardens are kept as grand as ever.* Opposite: *The verdant plantings almost obscure the graceful lines of this Garden District residence.*

This page, left: *If the Garden District seems captured in a more leisurely era, the vibrant Vieux Carré (New Orleans' French Quarter) is where the modern and historic meet face-to-face. Below: In the French Quarter itself, no building may be higher than the spire of St. Louis Cathedral, which overlooks Jackson Square, the heart of the district. Opposite: The shutter door is typical of the architectural detail in the French Quarter, the home of the restaurants, antique shops, and jazz venues that draw so many tourists. Overleaf: Built in the early 1800's on Key West for harbor pilot Captain John H. Geiger, this house was named Audubon House in honor of the great naturalist John James Audubon, who visited the island in 1832.*

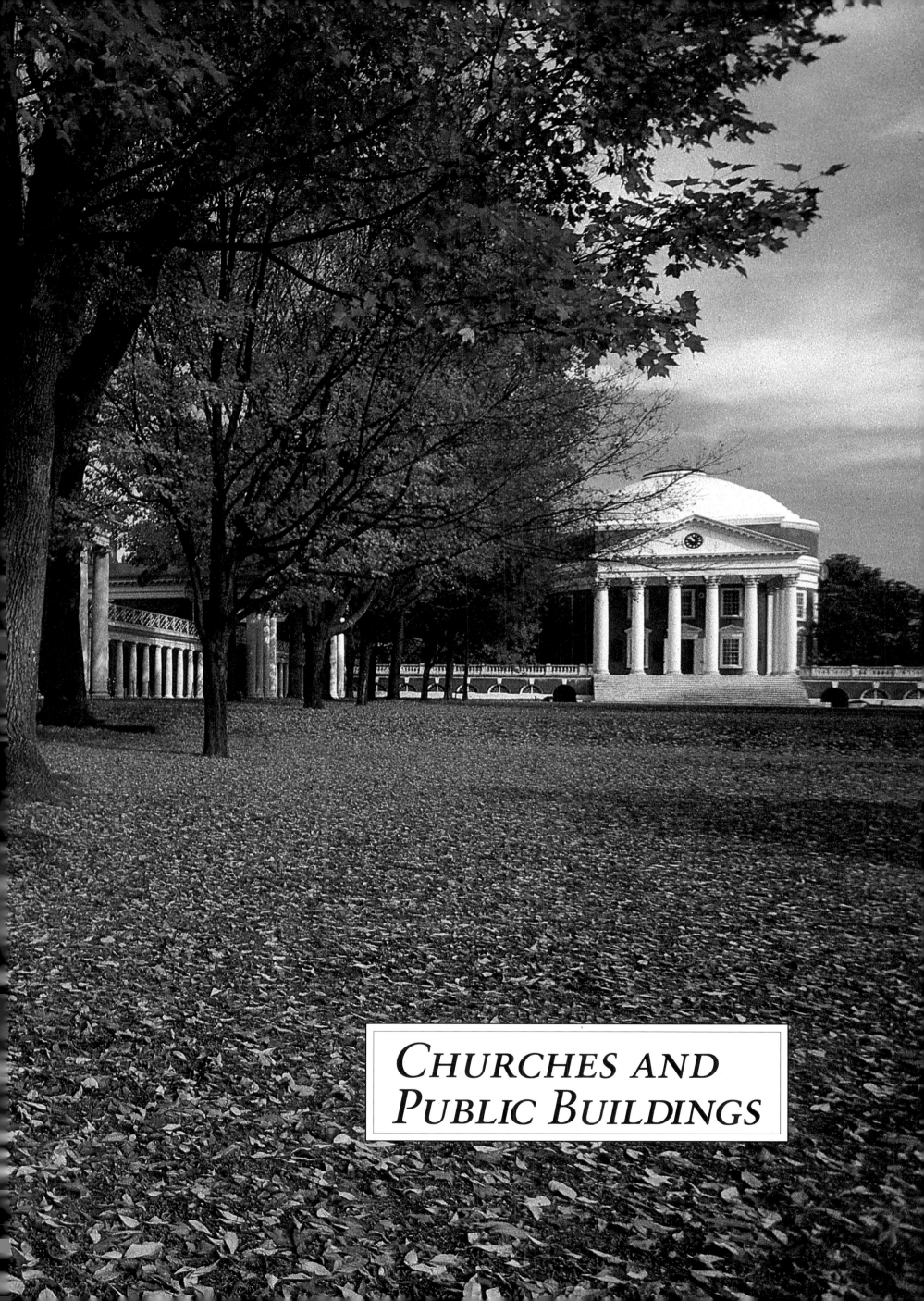

CHURCHES AND
PUBLIC BUILDINGS

Preceding pages: *The University of Virginia is one of Thomas Jefferson's greatest achievements. He created the school in 1819, selected a site just down the hill from his Monticello plantation, and designed the original campus as an "academical village" that still embodies the values of the Age of Enlightenment. This page, left: The Virginia capitol in Richmond, another of Jefferson's design gems, was closely modeled on a Roman temple at Nimes, France, and features the first interior dome built in the New World. Below: Abington, Virginia, just above the Tennessee border, was a jumping off point for families, including that of Daniel Boone, who were moving into the frontier; the town hall is pictured here.*

Preceding page: *The North Carolina State Capitol, a quintessential example of Greek Revival architecture, was built in 1840.* This page, left: *The monumental statue of George Washington gets pride of place in the North Carolina Capitol.* Below: *The state legislature met in these rooms until 1963, when it moved to a nearby building designed by Edward Durrell Stone. Now, the Senate chamber in the Old Capitol, restored to the way it looked 150 years ago, serves as a museum.*

This page, clockwise from left: *In 1837, the U.S. government opened its first branch mint in Charlotte, North Carolina, and coins were turned out here until 1913. The first three centuries of Charleston, South Carolina's history are outlined in a multimedia presentation in the Old Exchange, where Washington was but one of the famous visitors. On the second floor of Charleston's City Hall is a picture gallery of notables who visited the city; it includes prized portraits by John Trumbull (of Washington) and Samuel F.B. Morse (of Monroe). Following page: This Charleston courthouse, designed in 1789 by William Drayton, was one of the first buildings with a portico above an arched arcade and was a precursor of the White House.*

Preceding pages: *The shining white spire of this church on Broad Street towers above tropical vegetation.* This page, left to right: *The seal of the Church of Scotland over the main entrance identifies this 1814 building on Meeting Street as Charleston's First Scots Presbyterian Church. Services at the Huguenot Church were conducted in French until 1928; now English is used except for one Sunday each spring. At the end of the peninsula on which Charleston is built is White Point Gardens, from which visitors can view Fort Sumter.* Opposite: *The Farmers Society Hall in Pendleton, South Carolina, long served as a center for Oconee County's apple industry.* Following pages, left: *The Tennessee State Capitol, built with ornate decorations on the ironwork, is a prize example of the Greek Revival style.* Right: *William Strickland, who designed the Tennessee Capitol, is buried within the edifice.*

Preceding pages: *General James Oglethorpe, Georgia's founder, organized the nation's oldest Mason's lodge, which has been in continuous operation since 1734. Opposite: Tar, pitch, and similar naval stores, as well as cotton, were traded at the Cotton Exchange, which was the first building in the U.S. to use the legal concept of air rights to build above public space. This page, above: The Confederate Memorial Hall in Savannah keeps alive the memory of the secessionist movement. Below: Down Bay Street from the Cotton Exchange, each cotton broker had an office and warehouse; visitors still throng to Factor's Walk to see the way these buildings are connected to the river bluff by intricate iron bridges.*

This page, above: *The chapel of the University of Georgia, built in 1832, contains a 23-foot-long painting of the interior of St. Peter's Basilica in Rome.* Below: *From this residence, the University of Georgia president oversees a massive educational complex housing not only 25,000 students but also working farms, forest preserves, and a 293-acre botanical garden.*

This page, clockwise from left: *The first medical college in Georgia was chartered in 1828 and became operational when this Augusta building was opened in 1835. The Celtic Cross is one of the many mementoes of the past in Augusta, long an important trading center. Milledgeville served as Georgia's capital city from 1804 until after the Civil War; the Palladian governor's mansion was erected in 1839. Following page: The Confederate flag as well as that of the U.S. flies beneath the dome of Atlanta's Capitol, which is gilded with gold mined in Dahlonega, Georgia.*

Preceding pages, left: *The Mississippi Capitol from 1840 until 1903, this building at State and Capitol streets in Jackson now houses the State Historical Museum. Right: In the Old Capitol, dioramas trace the history of Mississippi. Also on display is a collection of materials associated with Confederate President Jefferson Davis. This page, above: The New Capitol in Jackson is modeled on the U.S. Capitol in Washington, although the reddish limestone gives a quite different effect. Left: The elaborate glass designs in the dome on the New Capitol are unassailable clues to the Beaux-arts spirit of the building.*

This page, above: *Andrew Jackson's victory over 10,000 British troops at the Battle of New Orleans assured his place as a hero; this square in New Orleans was renamed in his honor.* Right: *Clark Mills was the sculptor for the towering statue in the center of Jackson Square.* Overleaf: *Next to St. Louis Cathedral is the Cabildo, built in 1795 as the headquarters for the Spanish who then ruled Louisiana. It was in this building that the land bought in the Louisiana Purchase was turned over to the U.S.*

Above: *The "Napoleon House"—a private residence on Chartres Street—was bought by French loyalists as a refuge for the exiled emperor, but he died before they could put their rescue operation into effect. Below: Orleans and Royal are in the heart of the Vieux Carré, near such much-visited remnants of the Old South as the home of New Orleans architect John Gallier, Jr. and the shops of Brulatour Courtyard.*

Above: *The above-ground cemeteries are a distinctive feature of New Orleans, and a gold mine of information for genealogical researchers.* Below: *In the cemeteries, evidence of the diverse groups that formed New Orleans live on: the monuments recall Creole, Cajun, African, Caribbean, and British families.*

St. Charles Church in Grand Coteau in the middle of the Louisiana bayou country is a fitting reminder of the motivating role religion played in the history of the Old South.

The Southern Legacy

The history of the Old South from Jamestown to Appomattox, the heritage of the Washingtons and Lees and millions of others less famous, is still very much with us. John Hope Franklin, in *The Southerner as American,* describes the South as unique because it is "a section where the cult of history is so deeply embedded and where the past looms so large in the present."

It is characteristic of this region that the past is a vital part of the present, and its artifacts are proudly displayed in elaborately reconstructed historical districts and simple small-town museums. The novelist Eudora Welty captured the philosophy of her fellow southerners when she wrote, "One place comprehended can make us understand other places better. Sense of place gives equilibrium; extended, it is a sense of direction too." Today the relics and the wonders of the past which forged the present are spread out for all to see.

It is no accident that the first museum in this country was the Charleston Museum, opened in 1773 and today tracing through a cornucopia of furniture, silver, costumes, games, and photographs the exciting history of the South Carolina seaport. The movement to preserve for the public the homes of the most famous began with Mount Vernon in Virginia. The determined Ann Pamela Cunningham founded the Mount Vernon Ladies' Association, which took over the estate before the Civil War and manages it still. Contemporary urban preservationists take as their models the citizens who managed to keep vibrant the historical districts of Natchez, Richmond, Charleston.

Louisiana and South Carolina were pioneers in passing state laws to facilitate the retention and rehabilitation of historic buildings and neighborhoods. On the local level, the first city historical-preservation ordinance in the nation was enacted in Charleston in 1931; it "led the way for the development across the country of strong municipal preservation programs," says Stephen N. Dennis, a historian of the preservation movement.

Another prolific chronicler of the preservationists' efforts, Charles B. Hosmer, Jr., writes, "Americans were learning to define their history in a new way. It was to be a part of their living environment." He notes that in the two decades after the Charleston ordinance, "historical groups began to unite for the first time to save whole districts in a number of cities and small towns. The urban preservation movement seemed to center in the seaport and riverport communities of the South. The emphasis was nostalgic and centered on beautiful homes."

No place illustrates this better than Charleston, because no town of the Old South was more magnificent or richer in history. The way the historic district survived the terrible assault of Hurricane Hugo in late 1989 with only minimal damage is simply the most recent testimony to how well our forefathers constructed their dwellings. Hugo was the twentieth bona fide hurricane to hit the city since accurate record-keeping of wind speeds began in 1892.

The Charleston Museum, in addition to its own displays, now owns three fine mansions through which one can chart the development of the elegant life of the town from the earliest days of the republic. The Heyward-Washington House is the oldest of the trio. Built in 1772 by rice planter Daniel Heyward—whose son Thomas was a signer of the Declaration of Independence—it provided lodging for George Washington on his 1791 trip to the city and serves to show off the finest accomplishments of the early American furniture makers. The Joseph Manigault House of 1803 is a prize example of the influence of Robert Adam on American architects and delights visitors with its secret staircase connecting the second and third floors. The Aiken-Rhett Mansion was built in 1817 just two blocks from what was soon the site of the first railroad in the country; it still displays in some rooms the original wallpaper and paint, as well as a number of pieces of furniture that belonged to the original owners.

The special charm of Charleston is not just its showplaces but also the continued use of the buildings of more ordinary citizens. In all, more than 2,000 dwellings are now protected by the city's preservationists, and most of them are still in use as private homes. When developers threaten to raze an old house, the local establishment sees to it that the dwelling is moved to a new site where it can continue to function.

One can buy pottery today in a pink shop that was built in the seventeenth century of coral stone from the Caribbean islands and used as a sailors' tavern with one room per floor. Or attend a play in the Dock Street Theatre, a reconstruction of an early Georgian playhouse on the site. Or attend services in Kahal Kodosh Beth Elohim, the oldest synagogue in the United States in continuous use, the outgrowth of the Jewish community that first came to Charleston in 1670. Or visit the Thomas Elfe Workshop, where a mid-eighteenth-century craftsman constructed for himself an exact miniature of the homes of the Charleston rice aristocracy, complete with marvelous cypress paneling.

Not as glittering as Charleston, but equally as charming and as tangible an embodiment of the mythic South, Natchez also cherishes its architectural past. Sixty-four square blocks rising eastward from the Mississippi contain most of the 500 antebellum homes still standing in the city as well as such other early-nineteenth-century buildings as Meyer's Store, with its cast-iron Corinthian columns painted to look like marble, and the Trinity Episcopal Church, built in 1823 in a simpler style than its present incarnation. The great Doric portico that dominates the building was added more than a decade later.

At Eastertime and in mid-October, dozens of the Natchez residential gems that still serve as family homes are opened to the public. During the rest of the year, not only can their pristine facades be enjoyed from the street, but also a choice few have been made into museums that are open year-round. Many—including Monmouth, an 1818 Greek Revival home with most of its auxiliary buildings still intact, and Dunleith, set in 40 acres of wooded bayous—have arrangements for visitors to stay overnight. One of the most unusual Natchez houses, also taking overnight guests, is Ravennaside, built not for the family to live in but as a party house, where gala entertainments could be given; musicians played on a balcony overlooking the polished parquet floor of the ballroom.

But, as in Charleston, not all of the preservation reflects life at the top of the social pyramid. Below the bluff on which the town proudly stands is Natchez-under-the-Hill, where shortly after the Revolutionary War boatmen used to tie up for the night and outlaws on the run sought shelter. The neighborhood was famous throughout the South as the vice quarter, known as the "Sodom of the Mississippi." Few of the saloons of its early days remain, but at One Silver Street there still stands an inn that served as a famous bordello in the 1840's.

Raffishness has long been an important part of the heritage of New Orleans, where the enjoyment of life is a top priority. In a recent book, William Bryant Logan and Vance Muse note, "The city of New Orleans has been many things: a thoroughly European settlement yet a quintessentially American boomtown; a hedonistic colonial outpost (named for the depraved Duke of Orléans, Louis XV's powerful regent) and a Catholic stronghold; a steamy, tropical badland, twisted and teased into ordered gardens."

New Orleans is not encrusted in that history; it is a busy, working city, a center for booming international trade. Sited at the marshy confluence of the Mississippi River and the Gulf of Mexico, it has been subject to damaging floods, now largely controlled by a system of levees.

Benjamin Henry Latrobe, the architect who shaped the new nation's sense of self as supervising engineer of the construction of the public buildings in Washington, was mightily impressed with the distinctive look of New Orleans when he visited in 1819. Today many of the same buildings are still there: the Cabildo, from which the Spanish ruled Louisiana and the French turned over the territory to the United States; the nearby Presbytère, built in 1795 and for many years a courthouse; St. Louis Cathedral; the Ursuline Convent, originally dedicated in 1734 and now the home of the archdiocesan archives.

All those buildings are near neighbors in the Vieux Carré, a quarter that is a kind of huge museum, a live, throbbing museum. The evidence of the Old South on display there includes not only the jewels of the Spanish era but such other monuments as the Beauregard-Keyes House of 1826; the Hermann-Grima House, where Creole cooking demonstrations are given every Thursday on the open hearth in the outlying kitchen building; and the Italianate house at 1118 Royal Street, built in 1832 but now restored to the style of the Civil War era when it was the home of James Gallier, Jr., the architect of many of the most impressive houses in the Garden District.

A recent publication of the National Building Museum notes: "Structures are telling evidence of history. They can be significant as cultural artifacts, for their design, as examples of vernacular building types, or by association with an important individual or event." If Charleston, Natchez, and New Orleans serve as prime examples of historic preservation, the other way of continuing to appreciate the structures of the past—reconstruction—is best exemplified by Williamsburg, Virginia. The town was central to the history of the United States in the eighteenth century—the home of the second college in the colonies, the first Virginia newspaper, the House of Burgesses where Americans learned how a democratic legislature worked, and was little more than a village during the nineteenth century, after the state capital was moved to Richmond.

Today, its historic area—a mile long and a half-mile wide—is again the colonial capital of the 1750's, the result of more than 60 years of efforts by archaeologists and historians. The buildings that were still standing when the renewal effort began in 1926 have been refurbished, and well over 50 public buildings, stores, and houses have been built from scratch on the sites and in the styles of the colonial originals. Residents who stroll the 100-foot-wide Duke of Gloucester Street dressed in eighteenth-century garb on their way to work as guides or craftsmen in the blacksmith's, bookbinders', bootmakers', or wig shops add a living presence to the illusion. Well over 1 million visitors a year step back more than 200 years to savor both the glories and the hardships of early southern living.

The magic of Williamsburg is the way the restored and the reconstructed blend together. The two major buildings in the town—the Capitol with its twin rounded wings and delicate clocktower, and the Governor's Palace, dominating 10 acres of formal gardens—were built just before World War II. But visitors are looking at originals when they examine Bruton Parish Church, alongside the Palace grounds and in continuous use since 1715; the Magazine, where the Virginia militia stored their arms and where colonial weapons are still on display; and Wythe House, an in-town copy of a James River plantation homestead and the home of the man who taught law to Thomas Jefferson, John Marshall, and Henry Clay.

The buildings—the grand and the modest, the public and the private—blend together into a pleasing whole because they share a common sense of scale. "Williamsburg's builders were neither technical innovators nor decorative geniuses," Ernest M. Frank wrote while serving as Director of Architecture of Colonial Williamsburg. "They were competent craftsmen who did not look far beyond their immediate assignment of adapting English forms to a New World setting. If they had genius at all it was a genius of taste, an awareness that space and scale were tools that could be as useful as the pitsaw and the molding plane."

For some, the most lasting memory taken away from Williamsburg will be its elegance—perhaps the crystal chandelier hanging in the center of the circular chamber of the colonial General Court, or the elaborate ironwork gates to the grounds of the Governor's Palace, or the great four-poster bed elaborately carved of oak and sheathed in cream-and-crimson curtains of brocatelle. For others it will be a telling detail of the simpler life, like the startlingly modern intersecting X's that make up the stair rails of the Coke-Garrett House, or the pedimented gable of the tiny Prentis Store. But whatever it is, it is an authentic taste of life in the colonies more than two centuries ago.

But tapping into the continuing heritage of the Old South is not just a case of making a pilgrimage to the best-known sites and the lauded collections. Throughout the region, writes Gene S. Stuart of the National Geographic Society, "people looked backward and liked what they saw—in the folkways of an earlier America and in its architecture. In city after city decaying old neighborhoods—some dating back to colonial times—found strong voices for preservation. And the handsome old houses would be more than mere symbols of the past." From the Chesapeake to the mouth of the Mississippi, there are tiny treasures to cherish.

Edgefield, South Carolina, won't even show up in most guidebooks, but it is a charming—and typical—example of the way the South blends hundreds of years of history. The town square was first established in 1787; it is now dominated by the first Confederate monument erected in the state. The most impressive building on the square is the county courthouse, built in 1839 and created by Robert Mills, the South Carolina architect more famous as the architect of the Treasury and the Washington Monument in Washington, D.C. Named by the drovers who herded wild turkeys and pigs from Buncombe, North Carolina, in the eighteenth century, Buncombe Street leads out of the square. Today the street is the site of many impressive mansions, including Halcyon Grove, the home of Andrew Pickens, Jr., elected governor of South Carolina in 1816; the 1815 boyhood home of Preston Brooks, U.S. Congressman; Holmewood, constructed in 1820 and later the home of Francis Hugh Wardlaw, author of the Ordinance of Secession which on December 20, 1860, made South Carolina the first state to quit the Union; and, just across the road, Carroll Hill, home of James Parsons Carroll, one of the signers of the Ordinance. A dozen other elegant and historic antebellum houses are preserved on other Edgefield avenues.

Or consider Washington, Arkansas, a once prosperous town in the southwestern part of the state which is now a state park. The town served as the Confederate capital of Arkansas after the Union army captured Little Rock; the county courthouse where the legislature met was restored in 1929, the state's first expenditure on historic preservation. All along Franklin Street and the cross streets, visitors find restorations and reconstructions of structures typical of the town during the first half of the nineteenth century: the blacksmith shop where James Bowie's innovative knife design was first forged; Dr. James Alexander Lafayette Purdom's house, portraying the way medicine was practiced in the antebellum era; the 1845 Royston House, full of museum-quality Empire furniture; the Tavern Museum; the B. W. Edwards Weapons Museum, with its impressive collection of flintlocks and muskets. A half-dozen other houses of the period are undergoing restoration. And the town is alive with activities—from its spring jonquil festival to its October turkey shoot with muzzle loading rifles—that bridge the distance from the past to the present.

In Montgomery, Alabama, in the compact Old North Hull Street area just north of the capitol building, are no fewer than 27 beautifully restored structures. They range from an 1818 tavern to the magnificent Ordermann-Shaw House, built around 1850 in the Italianate style and furnished in the elegant town house style of that period. Included in the collection are examples of much more modest dwellings, too, such as the kind of log cabin in which the first pioneers lived and a "shotgun" cabin typical of the housing of blacks in southern cities. Elsewhere the city preserves St. John's Episcopal Church, where Jefferson Davis worshipped, and the Rice-Semple-Haardt House, built in 1855 in a dizzying variety of styles, with a Greek Revival portico on a basically Italianate house with the upper levels full of the gingerbread associated with the Gothic Revival.

The historic district in Blountville, Tennessee, is even older. Laid out in 1792, it was already a major relay station for stagecoaches heading west from Abington, Virginia, and many brick, frame, and even log houses of that period still stand today. The John Anderson Townhouse, built in 1811, is a fine restoration, but even more history is associated with the Old Deery Inn, built in the mid-1780's and over the years serving as overnight lodging for such stagecoach passengers as the Marquis de Lafayette, Prince Louis Philipe, Andrew Jackson, James K. Polk, and Andrew Johnson.

Often the destination for the history buff is not a whole community but a single shelter for the past. As antiquarian John Brooke writes, "Books and manuscripts can tell us a great deal about the past, but they cannot tell us everything. Material objects and the places where people lived may also tell us a great deal." The shape of the handle of a butter churn or the combs used to hold up a lady's hair can suddenly reveal details of an entire way of life. Museums provide a permanent home for such artifacts of our past that otherwise might be swept away and forgotten.

Near Seagrove, in north central North Carolina, is the Potters Museum, exhibiting the way the local clay has been fashioned by residents, from the original 1750 settlers through contemporary craftsmen. In Laurel, Mississippi, the Lauren Rogers Museum of Art boasts one of the country's finest collections of baskets. The National Knife Museum in Chattanooga displays thousands of the implements that were so much a symbol of manhood for every southern gent. The Grand Guitar Museum in Bristol, Virginia, is shaped like a guitar and contains more than 200 examples of the guitars, banjos, and related string instruments central to the sound of the Old South.

In Natchitoches, Louisiana, founded in 1714, the oldest permanent settlement in the territory acquired in the Louisiana Purchase, artifacts of local history are preserved in the Bayou Folk Museum, located in the restored home of writer Kate Chopin. One of the largest collections of Civil War materials in the world is in the Abraham Lincoln Museum in Harrogate,

Tennessee. Furnishings of the 1840's are lovingly preserved in a home of the period in Marianna, Florida. On Tangier Island in Virginia, the Hopkins & Bro. Store, despite being enshrined on the august rolls of official Historic Landmarks, is still a place to buy apples or thread or nutcrackers, much as it was when it opened in 1842.

Savannah pays homage to its history as a major port in the Ships of the Sea Museum on the waterfront, displaying more than 100 ship models. To see the vessels full-sized, visit the Confederate Naval Museum in Columbus, Georgia, where the exploits of the South's sea-faring warriors are commemorated; its most prized exhibit is the hull of the *Muscogee,* an iron-clad Civil War gunboat. In Kinston, North Carolina, see the remains of the *Neuse,* another Confederate ironclad, but one that never fired a shot: low rainfall in 1864 kept it from being floated down the Neuse River from the yard where it was built, and the following year Commander Joseph Price ordered it scuttled so it would not fall into the hands of advancing Union troops. The *Neuse* is positively modern compared with the vessel displayed 150 miles farther east, on the waterfront in Manteo: a 69-foot square-rigged sailing ship modeled on those used by the Elizabethan explorers, manned by costumed guides who discuss with visitors what life on the rolling Atlantic was like in the late sixteenth century.

In addition to the sites devoted specifically to preserving history, the art museums of the South also preserve and display evidence of the style of life in the hundred years before the Civil War. Outstanding examples are at the Virginia Museum of Fine Arts in Richmond. There, an extensive series of portraits shows the James River colonial gentry; one of the most interesting aspects of the collection is the great variety of styles. They range from naive primitive paintings to highly sophisticated works. Art expert Eloise Spaeth explains the origin of the portraits: "The tobacco boats plying between England and America carried planters to London on business. While there, they often seized the opportunity to sit for portraits. Those who didn't make London might send detailed descriptions of how they looked, or wished to look, and in a matter of months portraits were returned." Especially fine in the Richmond collection are the portraits of the Ambler family and one for which William Byrd sat while a schoolboy in England.

The equally important portrait collection at the Gibbes Art Gallery in Charleston contains significantly more paintings actually done in the South. The most famous of the artists represented is Thomas Sully—ten of his portraits are on the walls—who lived in Charleston between the ages of eight and 27, while his father was manager of the town's premier theater. Even more interesting than Sully's work, if less accomplished artistically, are the five pastels by Henrietta Johnston, including her portrait of Mary du Bose. She is not simply the South's first woman artist, but is probably the first person of either sex to earn a living in the New World as a painter. Johnston's husband fell overboard as the couple was traveling from Ireland to America in 1705 and although rescued, he was so shaken by the experience that he never fully recovered. It was Henrietta who supported the family with her delicate brushwork.

Beyond portraiture, the best examples of art that portray the working life of the South are available at the former Delgado Museum, now known as the New Orleans Museum of Art. Neither William A. Walker nor Richard Clague are names known to the casual museum-goer, but their scenes of workers picking cotton and other daily routines of plantation life give us a double view of the Old South, both in the activities they depict and in the insights they give into the aesthetic interests of their landed patrons.

The art museums also display fine examples of the decorative arts and household objects that added the grace notes to southern living. The profusion of Sandwich glass goblets in the Birmingham Museum of Art and the eighteenth-century Wedgwood in the Mint Museum in Charlotte convey the elegance of formal dining. At the McBurney Art Memorial in Atlanta all the major periods in decorative arts since 1620 are arrayed. In the exemplary Abby Aldrich Rockefeller Folk Art Collection in Williamsburg, masterpieces of craftsmanship come together in the salon moved intact from an early-nineteenth-century house in Wagram, North Carolina. Also in North Carolina, at Winston-Salem, is the Museum of Early Southern Decorative Arts, which contains superlative examples of cabinetry and needlework from seven states.

Houses of worship are especially rich repositories of the physical heritage of our past because their artifacts are cherished and, in many cases, used continuously for centuries. At Merchant's Hope, near Hopewell, Virginia, the Bible—a binding together of an Old Testament printed in 1640 with a New Testament printed a year earlier—was a personal gift from Queen Anne. Not far away, at the Hungar's Parish Church on the narrow Virginia peninsula between the Chesapeake and the Atlantic, the communion service is one donated to the parish by John Custis IV in 1742. Far more magnificent than these simple country churches, the Cathedral of the Immaculate Conception in Mobile, begun in 1835, boasts incredibly detailed stained-glass windows imported from Germany. The baptismal font in Trinity Cathedral in Columbia, South Carolina, is by noted American sculptor Hiram Powers. Mikveh Israel in Savannah still uses the torah scrolls brought by the German and Portuguese founders of the congregation in 1733; also on view are letters to the synagogue from Washington, Jefferson, and Madison.

Throughout the South, the documentary history of the early days is preserved in libraries that welcome equally the scholar and the casual visitor. One of the best collections of items outlining the history of the Confederacy is at the DuPont Library at the University of the South in tiny Monteagle, Tennessee. The files of the negotiations that led to the Louisiana Purchase are on display, along with a fascinating hoard of historic maps showing the growth of the city, in the Merieult House in New Orleans, itself an exquisite example of late-eighteenth-century domestic architecture. A fine collection of papers tracing the history of Georgia is housed in McElreath Hall, the headquarters of the Atlanta Historical Society. The Alabama Department of Archives in Montgomery is especially useful to those doing genealogical research, and the Friedman Library in Tuscaloosa is worth a visit merely to see the splendid Italianate home of 1862 in which it is housed.

With the long and lush growing season in the South and the region's cultural preference for drama and romance, gardens have long been a distinctive feature; today they give visitors as accurate a view of the life of previous centuries as do the nonliving artifacts. Only half humorously, William Nathaniel Banks, who maintains a 300-acre garden with Italian sculpture at his home in Newnan, Georgia, muses, "Probably the greatest reward of gardening in the South is character development. The southern gardener, if he survives, will acquire patience, humility, stoicism, and irrepressible optimism in the face of devastating odds. The climate in Dixie is notoriously capricious."

Nonetheless, not only do many of the southern houses have magnificent gardens, but there are as well magnificent displays of blooms that are a testimonial to the love of beauty for beauty's sake. As proof of the authenticity of this heritage, there is the Trustees' Garden in Savannah, on the site of the original experimental garden begun by Oglethorpe in 1733 with seeds he had brought from London's Chelsea Physic Garden in hopes of creating vineyards and crops of medicinal herbs in the New World. There is even an herb house in the garden which is probably the oldest building in Georgia still extant. Instead, of course, Georgia became famous for its peaches, and the peach trees in Trustees' Garden are said to be the original ones in the colony.

The botanical gardens in Birmingham have been described as "67 acres of horticultural heaven"; among the displays is a formal Japanese garden. Just west of Jackson, Mississippi, is Mynelle Gardens, with a thousand varieties of plants but perhaps most interesting for its tropical area, which hints of what the South looked like before the Europeans arrived. In Sumter, South Carolina, the Swan Lake Iris Gardens contrast the pastels of the irises and camellias with the onyx-black waters of the lake. Farther east in South Carolina, at Murrells Inlet, Brookgreen Gardens, on the grounds of an eighteenth-century rice plantation, features, among stands of native wildflowers, 450 works of figurative sculpture by famous American sculptors.

Another way to taste the reality of history is to wander through the South's burying grounds. One—Boiling Springs Memorial Cemetery in the hamlet of Lynhurst, South Carolina—is the final resting place of many soldiers killed in the Revolutionary War and the War of 1812. The Confederate Memorial Park in Clanton, Alabama, has graves of Civil War soldiers, a collection of mementoes in what was once the Confederate Soldiers' Home, and a network of hiking trails through its 100 wooded acres. The Andersonville National Cemetery in Georgia, begun to inter Union soldiers who died at the prison camp, now contains the graves of 16,000 Confederate soldiers as well; it has been designated a National Historical Site.

One of the most poignant southern cemeteries is just outside Franklin, Tennessee, the site of the massive Civil War battle in which five Confederate generals were slain. Alongside the McGavock family plot at Carnton Plantation is the final resting place of 1,481 Confederate soldiers, a location seemingly foreshadowed a half-century earlier when Randal McGavock gave his 1,000-acre plantation a name that in Gaelic means "assemblage of stones."

Not surprisingly, however, the South saves its greatest enthusiasm for the grace, charm, and majesty of its plantation houses, which for visitors today seem to suggest that a fairy-tale world of beauty did in fact exist in the cotton culture. 40 years ago, when they were co-editors of the *Ladies Home Journal,* Bruce and Beatrice Gould wrote: "Here in this country, instead of palaces, temples, tombs or cathedrals, the real historical monuments are the fine old homes that tell the history of our American people. They keep a personal and appealing record of the way people lived when the nation was young." In no region is that as true as in the South.

One of the oldest plantation houses still exhibits its former glory. This is Drayton Hall in South Carolina, begun in 1738, completed in 1742, and lived in by seven generations of the Draytons with none of the accoutrements of modern technology. They lived there without electricity, plumbing, or central heating; they were so dedicated to preserving their heritage that they never even repainted the original buff-colored interior walls. When Drayton Hall was opened to the public, a few modern conveniences were added to protect the house—the only one in the region to survive the Civil War—but the place still gives visitors an unadulterated look at eighteenth-century plantation life.

Drayton Hall's red brick (a native construction material, like everything in the residence except the English limestone used on the portico trim and the Caribbean mahogany paneling on the central stairwell) seems to glow pink in the right light. Now owned by the National Trust for Historic Preservation, the house, which is unfurnished, is an architectural museum displaying fine plaster moldings, intricate woodwork, and authentic interior painting.

The ornamentation is impressive in the absolute, but is even more awesome as the product of a country just emerging from the wilderness. On a single pillar, garlands emerge from a furl of carved leaves, entwine floor-to-ceiling, surround rosettes, and disappear into a shell bas-relief. In the second floor drawing room, the hand-carved family coat of arms in the triangular space created by pedimented gables over the fireplace moves beyond craftsmanship to art.

Drayton Hall is credited with being the seminal merging of two architectural styles: the elegant Italian villas created in the sixteenth century by Palladio and so admired by enlightened colonists, and the simple practicality of West Indian building that lifted houses on stilts to better catch breezes and protect against torrential floods. Twin staircases carry visitors up almost a story to the wide portico that shields the front door of the mansion, away from the road and facing the bright blue Ashley River. It is the first use of the two-story-high portico in the New World, and helps make Drayton Hall one of the grandest of the pre-Revolutionary planters' residences.

It was rice that provided the basis of the Drayton family fortune and that of the neighboring planters. But theirs was not a one-crop economy. Indigo was grown in response to a subsidy scheme developed by Britain so that it would not have to buy the dye for its seamen's uniforms from the colonies of its enemy, France. After the American colonies won independence and the subsidy disappeared, the planters turned from indigo to cotton as their alternative crop.

The Drayton family began its farming operations at Magnolia Plantation before 1680. The plantation house there was destroyed during the Civil War but until recently, members of the family lived in the replacement built after the conflagration, and that home, and its 50 acres of lawn and garden, is also now open to the public.

Another of the Old South's land-owning dynasties created Houmas House, perhaps the gem of the string of Mississippi River plantation mansions southeast of Baton Rouge. Richard Pratt, who has written so many books about old American homes, calls Houmas House "one of the greatest."

Like so many others, the house evolved over the decades. The visitor today sees an elegant pillared white square with rounded dormers peeping out of the hip roof, set amid the moss-hung live oaks, absolutely prototypical of its neighborhood—and of the atmosphere that made the producers of the movie *Hush, Hush, Sweet Charlotte* decide to film the gothic tale there. Nearby are Bocage, Belle Hélène, Nottoway (with 64 rooms, the largest plantation house of them all), Tezcuco, and a half-dozen other survivals of the plantation houses that supported a busy Creole social whirl in the mid-nineteenth century. So leisured was the life there that servants rowed family members around in gilded barges and in summer the water from the Mississippi was cooled with ice for the morning baths.

This was the center of sugarcane production in America, which nurtured a distinctive way of life. The plantations were self-contained hamlets, the main house was flanked by offices, guest houses, and, typically, a *garçonnière* for the young bachelors who congregated there and were so essential to the success of dances and parties. (At Houmas House, the bachelor's annex is octagonal, with the ground floor nothing but a series of arches and the bedrooms on the second floor.) In back of the main house would be gardens, a carriage house, and perhaps fanciful dovecotes. In the front was the view—the mighty Mississippi. One English

visitor to Houmas House wrote back to friends, "If an English horticulturist could see 6,000 acres of the finest land in one field, unbroken by hedge and sprouting sugar cane, as level as a billiard table, he would surely doubt his senses." In fact, at its peak Houmas House saw 12,000 acres in cultivation.

Houmas House is a textbook example of the architectural style known as Louisiana Classic, an adaptation of Greek Revival to the humid heat of the region. The large attic gives insulation from the sun. The rooms have high ceilings; most of them open both to the central hall and to the gallery that surrounds the house on both the ground and upper floors, catching whatever breeze plays by and giving every resident access to the outdoors.

It took a long time for Houmas House to achieve this look. The first settler bought the land from the Houmas Indians in the 1700's and built what was in essence a French country villa, although with clear evidence of local Spanish influence. That structure is still in use, the rear appendage of the grander Louisiana Classic home. Wade Hampton, the Revolutionary War general from South Carolina who became the South's wealthiest planter, bought it for $300,000 ($100,000 of that in immediate cash) in 1812, to serve as the western headquarters of his vast holdings. (Hampton bought and sold land so fast that it was difficult to keep track of just what he owned at any given moment, but at the turn of the century his holdings probably added up to 7 million acres in a half-dozen states, as well as toll bridges and ferries.)

Later, title to the Louisiana property passed to Hampton's son-in-law, John Smith Preston, who oversaw the conversion of the French chateau into a sugarland mansion. Preston later sold the home for $1.5 million—an astounding price for the 1850's—to John Burnside, for whom the nearby village is named. That sale may have been the house's salvation, for Burnside was an Irishman and when Union troops marched through the area in the Civil War he insisted—successfully—that as a foreigner he did not have to comply with their demands to turn over the plantation to them.

So the home survives to delight visitors today, with original American-crafted furniture; hinges, door knobs, tiles, and ceiling sconces imported from France and Germany; and a sweeping curved central staircase that seems made for the rustle of silk and crinoline. The master bedroom is on the ground floor, immense with the scarlet of the brocaded canopy bed matched in the design of the Persian carpet on the floor. French porcelain vases adorn the mantelpieces in the twin parlors, and brass gleams on the table in the dining room, done in Spanish provincial style.

Unlike Houmas House, developed over decades, another of the best of the remaining plantation houses was created in one unified vision. Sweeping in an arc around a lush green lawn, the columned yellow-and-white Greek Revival beauty of Gaineswood in central western Alabama is enough to take one's breath away. It seems the embodiment of a culture that southerners found worth fighting to preserve. It was carefully designed, and constructed over almost two decades, to be just such a dream come true.

In 1843, General Nathan Bryan Whitfield bought from Indian agent George Gaines the land on which Gaineswood now sits; it was a leap of faith, for the largely undeveloped area was truly a rude frontier. As Roger Kennedy of the Smithsonian Institution notes, "the standard of living of Westerners nearly always dropped below what it had been in the East, and often stayed low for many years before it rose again. The hope, and the general experience, was that it would rise much higher, if not in the first generation, then in the next." There was a two-room log cabin on the land when Gaines sold it, but as Kennedy says, Whitfield "lived to see family portraits taken down from the pegs driven into log walls and rehung from the freshly painted cornices of a mansion."

Gaineswood has 20 rooms, today furnished with many of the pieces that Whitfield acquired while he was creating the estate between 1843 and 1860. Whitfield traveled widely and ordered from the best craftsmen throughout the growing nation furniture and wallpaper and such decorative accents as the silver doorknobs. And the family portraits do in fact hang on the walls in locations of honor. Gaineswood has been rated "one of the three or four most interesting houses in America."

The mirrored ballroom is as astonishing today as it must have been to the antebellum society that visited here. The lace curtains cascading down the tall windows of the drawing room capture the sense of romance and fantasy, and the light pouring in through the domed skylight in the dining room makes the tableware shimmer.

Whitfield himself gets most of the credit for Gaineswood. He was not only the inspiration and prod, but did most of the architectural detailing himself. Fascinated by mechanics— he invented the flutina, a mechanically driven musical instrument which is a sort of second cousin to the organ and one of the unique items still on display at the mansion—he even designed the lathes and routers needed to cut the intricate cornices, moldings, and pilasters that adorn the first floor public rooms. Somehow, the elaborate intertwined flowers work with the austere shell design inside the ceiling coffers and the baroque capitals look just fine atop the classic Greek columns.

Whitfield's main architectural influence came from Charles and James Dakin, who dominated public architecture in bustling Mobile, 100 miles down the Tombigbee River from Gaineswood, in the era when Gaineswood was being developed. A former associate of the Dakin brothers, Minard Lafever, had moved to New York and become the premier designer of interior wall and ceiling detailings. Whitfield bought some millwork created to Lafever designs and also had local craftsmen copy from pattern books published by Lafever.

At Gaineswood and Houmas House and Drayton Hall, the South of *Gone With the Wind* comes to life. Here is a place where once upon a time women abloom in gorgeous gowns swirled around the ballrooms on the arms of gallant men impeccable in dress and deportment. Here is a place where there was time on a sunny afternoon to read poetry and on a starry night to listen to singing carried by the night wind over the fields. Here is a place where civility was required and beauty cherished; where duty was an imperative and honor a way of life.

A myth? A creation of the fiction-makers? The evidence of the Old South that still exists today lets us think perhaps not.

Opposite: *Battle reenacters like this one must find their own uniforms and weapons. They often perform as extras in historical films as well as for the sheer enjoyment of it.*

SOLDIERS, FORTS, AND BATTLEFIELDS

This page, clockwise from left: *The 95-foot-tall Victory Monument stands at Yorktown, Virginia, site of the British surrender that secured independence for the U.S. The fortifications built by the British at Yorktown in 1781 were strengthened and used again by the Confederate army 80 years later. Visitors to the Yorktown battlefield can see the sections manned by troops under the various allied generals: Washington, Lafayette, Rochambeau, and von Steuben. Opposite: In tourist season, the decisive Yorktown battle is reenacted by dedicated history buffs, including these members of the "First Virginia Regiment."*

This page, above: *Petersburg, Virginia, hosts a reenactment of the epic Civil War battle of April, 1865, in which General Robert E. Lee's supply routes were cut, making his surrender the following week inevitable. Below: Petersburg National Battlefield preserves 1,600 acres of the historic site, and shows the fortifications of both the Confederate and Union troops. Opposite: Although defeated in the Civil war, the Confederacy today emerges as the more heroic side in modern reenactments of the decisive encounters.*

The battle at Sailors' Creek, Virginia, provides the script for one of the most exciting reenactments.

Crowds at Sailors' Creek cheer when the Confederate Stars and Bars emerges from the smoke of battle.

This page, above: *As the site of two major Civil War engagements 13 months apart, Manassas, Virginia, is one of the most popular destinations for history enthusiasts. Below: The McLean House in Appomattox, Virginia, is a faithful reconstruction of the home where Lee and Grant met on April 9, 1865 to sign the document ending the Civil War. Opposite: It was at the first Battle of Bull Run—the first major encounter of the Civil War—that the tenacity of Thomas J. Jackson earned him the nickname "Stonewall."*

THOMAS JONATHAN
JACKSON
1824
1863

"THERE STANDS JACKSON LIKE A STONE

This page: *Fort Macon is just one of the many examples of historic preservation in the coastal area around Beaufort, North Carolina.* Opposite: *Although silent now, the cannons at Fort Macon boom in the memories of visitors.*

This page, left: *In March 1781, the War for Independence was almost ended at the battle of Guilford Courthouse in North Carolina, where American troops under General Nathaniel Greene eliminated one-quarter of the British army under Cornwallis. Below: The military park at Guilford preserves the story: Greene held back from the final charge that would have forced Cornwallis to surrender, but the victory set the stage for the final battle at Yorktown in October 1781. Opposite: The victory commemorated at Kings Mountain, South Carolina, is important for its impact on the Revolutionary War. The British southern campaign was broken here in 1780; the Americans reported only 28 dead and 62 wounded in this action while all 1,100 soldiers under British Major Patrick Ferguson were killed or captured.*

This page, above: *Hand-hewn fortifications give contemporary visitors some insight into the bravery of the men who stood defense in these primitive forts.* Below: *Fort Sumter in Charleston has assured its place in history as the site where the first shells of the Civil War were fired.* Opposite: *Soldiers of both sides are remembered in the monuments commemorating the "Battle Above the Clouds" on Lookout Mountain, Chattanooga, Tennessee.* Following pages, left: *The preservation of key Civil War battlefields—such as this one at Kennesaw Mountain near Marietta, Georgia, also protects from development some of the loveliest scenery in the Old South.* Right: *Built overlooking Matanzas Bay in what is now St. Augustine, Florida, the Castillo de San Marcos was begun in 1672 as Spain's northernmost American outpost.*

Preceding pages: *The fortification also served as a British prison during the Revolutionary War, a Confederate stronghold during the Civil War, and, as Fort Marion, a U.S. Army base until it was designated a national monument in 1924. The Castillo is built of mollusk shells and sand. This page, above: Once known as the "Gibraltar of the Gulf," Fort Jefferson was the largest of the forts with which the U.S. ringed its eastern and southern coasts. Below: The impressive battlement on Garden Key still draws visitors to Fort Jefferson, even though it can be reached only by boat or seaplane. Opposite: Spanish pirates controlled the Dry Tortugas until 1821, and U.S. dominion was not really established until Fort Jefferson was begun in 1846. However, it was left uncompleted when yellow fever and hurricanes forced abandonment of the task nearly 30 years later.*

Preceding pages, left: *At South Royal and Church Street in the heart of modern downtown Mobile, Alabama, a reconstruction of Forte Condé, with workable reproductions of the kind of cannon used by the French Navy in the 1740's, serves as a visitor's center. Right: Forte Condé, modeled on the French headquarters built on the waterfront site in 1724, today houses a collection of muskets and other eighteenth-century armaments. This page: For months in 1862, Confederate control of Vicksburg, Mississippi, denied Union troops the use of the Mississippi River. When General Ulysses S. Grant laid siege to the town, the citizenry held out for a month before finally surrendering on July 4.*

Vicksburg is built on soft soil made of compacted silt, which made it easy for Confederate and Union troops to dig personal trenches.

This page, above: *Monuments honoring the fallen from both armies dot the former battlefield, now designated the Vicksburg National Military Park and Cemetery. Below: An unknown Union soldier killed in the battle at Vicksburg lies in this grave. Opposite: Inside the Illinois Memorial at Vicksburg, bronze tablets carry the name of each soldier from that state who fought in the encounter. Overleaf: The frieze on a battlefield monument at Vicksburg symbolizes both the reunion of the once rent nation, and the handshake of brotherhood essential to rebuilding and maintaining the South.*

INDEX OF PHOTOGRAPHY

TIB indicates The Image Bank.